Research & Education Association

The Best Teachers' Test Preparation for the

CSET®
English
Subtests I–IV

With REA's TEST*ware*® on CD-ROM

David Rosen, M.A.
Citrus College
Glendora, California

And the Staff of
Research & Education Association

Visit our Educator Support Center at:
www.REA.com/teacher

The content specifications for the CSET: English Subtests I-IV were created and implemented by the California Commission on Teacher Credentialing in conjunction with National Evaluation Systems, Inc., a unit of Pearson Education, Inc. For further information visit the CSET® website at *http://www.cset.nesinc.com*.

For all references in this book, CSET® and California Subject Examinations for Teachers® are trademarks of the California Commission on Teacher Credentialing and Pearson Education, Inc.

Research & Education Association
61 Ethel Road West
Piscataway, New Jersey 08854
E-mail: info@rea.com

**The Best Teachers' Test Preparation for the
California CSET®: English Subtests I–IV
with TEST*ware*® on CD-ROM**

Printed in the United States of America

Library of Congress Control Number 2007941775

ISBN-13: 978-0-7386-0377-3
ISBN-10: 0-7386-0377-5

Windows® is a registered trademark of Microsoft Corporation.

REA® is a registered trademark of
Research & Education Association, Inc.

About Research & Education Association

Founded in 1959, Research & Education Association is dedicated to publishing the finest and most effective educational materials—including software, study guides, and test preps—for students in middle school, high school, college, graduate school, and beyond.

REA's Test Preparation series includes books and software for all academic levels in almost all disciplines. Research & Education Association publishes test preps for students who have not yet entered high school, as well as for high school students preparing to enter college. Students from countries around the world seeking to attend college in the United States will find the assistance they need in REA's publications. For college students seeking advanced degrees, REA publishes test preps for many major graduate school admission examinations in a wide variety of disciplines, including engineering, law, and medicine. Students at every level, in every field, with every ambition can find what they are looking for among REA's publications.

REA's practice tests are always based upon the most recently administered exams and include every type of question that you can expect on the actual exams.

REA's publications and educational materials are highly regarded and continually receive an unprecedented amount of praise from professionals, instructors, librarians, parents, and students. Our authors are as diverse as the fields represented in the books we publish. They are well-known in their respective disciplines and serve on the faculties of prestigious high schools, colleges, and universities throughout the United States and Canada.

Today, REA's wide-ranging catalog is a leading resource for teachers, students, and professionals.

We invite you to visit us at *www.rea.com* to find out how REA is making the world smarter.

Acknowledgments

We would like to thank Larry Kling, Vice President, Editorial, for his overall direction; Pam Weston, Vice President, Publishing, for setting the quality standards for production integrity and managing the publication to completion; John Cording, Vice President, Technology, for coordinating the design, development, and testing of REA's TEST*ware*® software; Alice Leonard, Senior Editor, for project management and preflight editorial review; Diane Goldschmidt, Senior Editor, for post-production quality assurance; Heena Patel, Software Project Manager, for software testing; Christine Saul, Senior Graphic Artist, for cover design; and Jeff LoBalbo, Senior Graphic Artist, for post-production file mapping.

We also gratefully acknowledge Pennie Magee, Ph.D., of Rocky Mountain Publishing Professionals Guild for developmental editing; Kathy Caratozzolo of Caragraphics for typesetting and Stephanie Reymann for indexing the manuscript.

About the Author

I began my teaching career in the late 1970's with illustrating and drawing classes. I earned my Master's degree in English at the University of Oregon. I'm currently an English instructor at Citrus Community College in Glendora, California, though home is Eugene, Oregon. I've taught at Fullerton College, Murray State College, and the University of Oregon. I am a former director for a teacher recruitment program. My proudest academic accomplishment came as a result of the two consecutive years my students selected me as "their most influential teacher."

Concurrently, I'm a freelance writer/editor, writing and editing academic materials for companies like REA and Greenwood Press. I've also served as a consultant, aiding in the design and successful implementation of a private preparatory school's English curriculum.

I'm also a fine artist, a photographer, and a rank amateur guitar player. Primarily, if it involves the fine arts in some way, I'm there.

David Rosen

Contents

CONTENTS

Foreword

Let's face it: A five-hour test makes for a long day of testing. And it's a test you need to pass, because more than a letter grade hangs in the balance. This can equal some pretty intense anxiety when it comes to taking the California Subject Examinations for Teachers (CSET): English. But if you're taking the CSET: English Test, then you've already taken plenty of exams in the past, and this one is no different. Think of it as a couple of two-hour finals back-to-back. Better yet, think of it as four one-hour finals back-to-back. You may notice that I'm not a mathematician—it's actually a five-hour test. But thinking of each of the four sections as a separate course of study will help you focus your preparation.

The four topic sections covered on the CSET are literature, language, composition, and communications. The questions in each section will evaluate your level of understanding through the application of critical-thinking techniques. The sections are like an introductory or survey course; each section will cover a broad cross-section of information pertaining to that particular subject. At the same time, the questions in each section will ask you to apply your knowledge to a particular text, author, genre, and so on. Thus, for example, English Subtest I: Literature and Textual Analysis might ask you questions ranging from "Who wrote *The Adventures of Huckleberry Finn*?" to "What are the components of an epic?" and "Discuss the thematic representation of a Native American poem."

Each section follows suit. English Subtest II: Language, Linguistics, and Literacy will address your understanding of topics such as how indigenous, international, and historical languages develop; how vowels are formed in the mouth and throat; and at what age children develop the skills to read and comprehend certain information. This section will also include questions pertaining to the rules of grammar and syntax.

CSET Tip

Keep your response simple, brief, and to the point.

English Subtest III: Composition and Rhetoric will ask you to write an expository essay in response to a sample reading. The sample might be a poem, a couple of prose paragraphs, or an article; your goal in this section is to write a simple, clear, objective, and most important, thoughtful essay. This is the section where you'll want to revert back to those basic composition fundamentals such as an introduction with a clearly defined

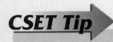

CSET Tip

Focus on the essentials of writing rather than on interpreting the passage.

thesis (a topic and claim), a body of support taken from the text (quotes, etc.), and a conclusion (paraphrase/summary of your thesis). The guiding principle for this section is: *Don't get fancy!* Keep your response simple, clear, brief, and to the point. Introduction, body, conclusion—that's it. Remember, you are *not* being asked to write your dissertation or show your brilliance. You are being asked to demonstrate your understanding of basic composition fundamentals, so less is more. Don't overthink the test question and don't overthink your response to the literary passage. Answer as clearly as you can and focus more on the essential compositional components that go into writing a successful literary response paper than on your interpretation of thematic elements.

English Subtest IV: Communications: Speech, Media, and Creative Performance will test your understanding of basic journalism techniques such as effective interview and reporting strategies. Then you'll be asked to respond to questions such as "What makes an effective oral presentation?" "What are the fundamentals of successful theatrical production and performance?" and "What are the components of creative writing?"

Notice that if you think of each section summarized in simple terms—section 1 is Literature; section 2, Literacy; section 3, Composition; and section 4, Communications—then preparing for them becomes the equivalent of studying for a generalized final exam.

If you don't know already, you'll soon discover in which areas you're strongest and in which areas you'll need to spend more review and practice time. If you've saved old course material(s), now's the time to get them out of mothballs and review the fundamentals as they were presented to you in class. You'll be amazed how much will come back to you once you see the information scribbled in your own handwriting. And for those people who are reading this and thinking to themselves, "Darn! I knew I should have saved that school stuff!", not to worry. There is a list of books at the end of this manual to help you fill in the gaps, and local libraries (public or academic) will have all the study materials you'll need. In addition, websites such as the following offer good academic information, and provide you with the opportunity to review writing fundamentals and receive immediate feedback:

Purdue University's Online Writing Lab (OWL): *http://owl.english.purdue.edu*

Washington State University's OWL: *http://owl.wsu.edu/*

Carnegie Mellon University's "Advice on Research and Writing" page: *http:// www.cs.cmu.edu/afs/cs.cmu.edu/user/mleone/web/how-to.html*

University of Ottawa's "HyperGrammar" course: *http://www.uottawa.ca/academic/ arts/writcent/hypergrammar/*

Interactive writing and grammar exercises, printable exercises, and interpretive samples combined with a variety of technical and professional writing resource links make Purdue's OWL a particularly valuable resource. And the best part is that access to the websites listed here and others like them is free. A few visits will refresh your memory about the basics of writing. So whether you've saved your school notes or not, head for library and academic writing lab websites, and begin reviewing the basics. (A note about commercial websites: Commercial websites are retail websites. That is, they want to sell you something. A commercial site has *.com* at the end of its address, as in *www.amazon. com*. Websites maintained by organizations such as the Humane Society of the United States [www.hsus.org] and Project Gutenberg [www.gutenberg.org] are designated with an *.org* at the end of their addresses, and academic institutions such as the University of Oregon [www.uoregon.edu] are designated with an *.edu* ending.

TEST-TAKING TIPS

Read each test question slowly and carefully. Don't let the adrenaline push you to work too fast. Even the best writers will make the dumbest mistakes when feeling pressured or tired. You will note that the scored responses in the "Sample Essays" sections of Practice Tests 1 and 2 share similar characteristics. The four- and three-point responses all directly answer the questions with clear vocabulary and critical reasoning, while the two- and one-point responses include all the dumb mistakes we can make when we hurry to start (or finish) writing rather than taking the time to think. If you get too far ahead of yourself, you're liable to make mistakes such as writing *their* when you mean *they are*, or *your* for *you are* and *its* for *it is*, and so on. You may find yourself writing mundane phrases, dangling your modifiers, or using abstract language in place of concrete terminology. Or perhaps you'll simply forget what verb tense you're in. Dumb mistakes don't just happen to the kids who slept through composition class; every writer makes them when he or she tries to write before thinking. So constantly monitor your pace, especially in the essay sections. Remember to keep it slow and steady or you'll lose your mental focus. Stop and check yourself periodically to see if your arms are tense or if your jaw, neck, or shoulders are knotted up. If they are, take a breath, stretch, flex, or shake out your tight muscles—

whatever it takes to relax them. Most important, pay attention to whether you're hurrying to write down your thoughts before you forget them; preferably, you will be developing your thoughts completely and then writing them down. If you remember to stay grounded and not succumb to the rush of adrenaline during the test, your perceptions and writing skills will improve significantly.

CSET Tip

Stay grounded and your perceptions will improve.

DEALING WITH TEST ANXIETY

One of my more inspiring students insists that I include my "notes on overcoming test anxiety" in any test-related materials I write, so this is for him.

Okay, first things first: what is test anxiety? Well, anyone who's ever cared about how well they do on an exam knows what test anxiety is. It's that nervous, noxious, nauseous worry that builds up in your gut, usually the night or so before a big test. Essentially, it's the self-imposed stress, pressure, and tension that makes you worry, shake, and sweat, and that can result in you forgetting what you already know.

So, now the question becomes "How do I overcome this test anxiety?" and the answer begins with a remarkably simple premise: Remember, you already know what's on the test. Think about it for a minute—it's true. If you've been awake at all in your classes, if you've done the reading, perhaps written in a journal, listened to the lectures, asked questions, done research, worked in an academic environment, or participated in any of the other various educational endeavors that have likely gotten you to this point, you've already encountered and addressed the materials that are going to be on the test. So, rather than worry about what you won't remember, or what may or may not be on the exam, simply remind yourself, starting as soon as possible before test day, that you already know what's on the test and that you've already handled it in one form or another. It's really nothing more than a review of the materials you've already covered somewhere in your academic life.

It might also help you to know that nearly 99 percent of your professors devise their tests from the books and materials that they've gone over in class lectures. And yes, you'll always have that infamous 1 percent of the faculty who'll ask you questions from left field like "What did Pierre d'Aubusson have for breakfast the morning he battled the

Ottoman Empire?" or "If you were stranded on a deserted island, which Atomic Rooster CD would you want to have and why?" but those professors are the exceptions rather than the rule. The majority of instructors create tests from the materials in the books, and most textbooks conform to state and federal academic assessment guidelines and criteria, the same guidelines and criteria that the CSET is built upon. Thus, in a not so roundabout way, you've already been presented with the majority of materials you'll encounter on the test.

So relax, and keep reminding yourself that you already know the material. Do this repeatedly during the course of each day, starting weeks before the test if possible. And when you encounter that 1 percent of the questions that seems off the wall, you'll just give it the best educated guess you can and then move on to the next question, which most likely will be one whose answer you already know.

I can't stress enough how important this positive reinforcement technique is, or how much better you'll perform as a result of practicing it. All I ask is that you give it a try and see if it works for you. I'm confident you'll see and feel the results immediately.

Remember that many have traveled this road before you and lived to tell the tale. While taking the CSET is one of the arduous steps required on the road to a career in education, the rewards are more than worth the effort. If others can do it, you can too! As you review the material and take the practice tests in this book, remember to keep the test in perspective. There will be a time in the not too distant future when you will be telling your students about a career in education. When one of them asks you about taking exams such as the CSET, you may even smile and tell them, "It wasn't so bad."

Good luck.

Introduction
Passing the CSET: English Test

ABOUT THIS BOOK AND TESTware®

REA's *The Best Teachers' Test Preparation for CSET: English Subtests I-IV* is a comprehensive guide designed to assist you in preparing for an English educator license in California. To enhance your chances of success in this important step toward your career as an English teacher, this test guide along with REA's exclusive TEST*ware*®:

• Presents an accurate and complete overview of the four CSET subtests

• Identifies all of the important information and its representation on the test

• Provides a comprehensive review of every domain on the test

• Provides two full-length practice tests

• Suggests tips and strategies for successfully completing standardized tests

• Replicates the format of the official tests, including levels of difficulty

• Supplies the correct answer and detailed explanations for each question on the practice tests, which enable you to identify correct answers and understand why they are correct and, just as important, why the other answers are incorrect.

This guide is the result of studying many resources. The editors considered the most recent test administrations and professional standards. They also researched information from the California Commission on Teacher Credentialing (CCTC), professional journals, textbooks, and educators. This guide includes the best test preparation materials based on the latest information available.

ABOUT THE TEST

CSET: English consists of four separate subtests, each scored separately and composed of either multiple-choice, constructed-response, or short-response questions. This English test represents the combined expertise of California educators, subject area specialists, and district-level educators who worked to develop and validate the test. This book contains a thorough review of each subtest, as well as the specific skills that demonstrate each content domain.

Who Administers the Test?

All the CSET tests are administered by National Evaluation Systems, Inc. (NES) and the CCTC. See contact information below.

Can I Retake the Test?

The CSET can be taken as many times as needed to achieve a passing score. Note: Once you pass a subtest, you do not have to take that subtest again, as long as you use the score toward certification within five years of the test date.

When Should the CSET Be Taken?

Candidates are typically nearing completion of or have completed their undergraduate work when they take CSET tests.

CSET tests are administered six times a year at 26 locations in California and five locations in other states. To receive information on upcoming administrations of the CSET, consult the CSET test date chart at the CSET website. For all information:

> CSET Program
> National Evaluation Systems
> P.O. Box 340789
> Sacramento, CA 95834-0789
> Telephone: (916) 928-4003 (9:00 a.m.–5:00 p.m. Pacific Time, Monday-Friday)
> Automated Information System: (800) 205-3334 (available 24 hours daily)
> Website: *http://www.cset.nesinc.com*

Is There a Registration Fee?

To take any CSET test there is a fee. It is structured per subtest. A complete summary of the registration fees is included in the CSET Registration Bulletin at the website above.

FORMAT OF CSET: ENGLISH

CSET: English assesses the candidate's proficiency and depth of understanding of the foundations of the subject contained in the English Content Standards for California Public Schools.

You are given five hours to complete the test, whether you take one or all of the subtests during one testing session. By monitoring your progress on the practice tests and adding one test at a time, you can reach your own comfort level and approach your testing session with confidence.

The following chart is a clear representation of the subtests and their domains and approximate number of questions.

Subtest	Domains	Number of Multiple-Choice Questions	Number of Constructed-Response Questions
I*	Literature & Textual Analysis	40	none
	Composition & Rhetoric	10	
	Subtest Total	50	none
II	Language, Linguistics, and Literacy	50	none
	Subtest Total	50	
III	Composition & Rhetoric and Literature & Textual Analysis	none	Subtest III consists of 2 constructed-response questions—1 based on literary text, 1 on nonliterary text. (extended responses)
IV	Communications: Speech, Media, & Creative Performance	none	4 (short responses)

*Subtest I is a multiple-choice test that covers the two domains of Literature & Textual Analysis and Composition & Rhetoric. Subtest III is a constructed-response test that covers the same domains.

HOW TO USE THIS BOOK AND TEST*ware*®

How Do I Begin Studying?

Identify which CSET: English subtest you wish to prepare for, then review the organization of this test preparation guide.

1. To best utilize your study time, follow our CSET Independent Study Schedule. The schedule is based on a six-week program, but can be condensed if necessary.

2. Take the first practice test for each subtest on CD-ROM, score it according to directions, then review the explanations to your answers carefully. Then, study the areas that your scores indicate need further review.

3. Review the format of the CSET.

4. Review the test-taking advice and suggestions presented later in this section.

5. Pay attention to the information about the objectives of the test.

6. Spend time reviewing topics that stand out as needing more study.

7. Take the second practice test for each subtest on CD-ROM and follow the same procedure as #2 above.

8. Follow the suggestions at the end of this section for the day before and the day of the test.

When Should I Start Studying?

It is never too early to start studying for the CSET. The earlier you begin, the more time you will have to sharpen your skills. Do not procrastinate!

A six-week study schedule is provided at the end of this section to assist you in preparing for the CSET: English. This schedule can be adjusted to meet your unique needs. If your test date is only four weeks away, you can halve the time allotted to each section, but keep in mind that this is not the most effective way to study. If you have several months before your test date, you may wish to extend the time allotted to each section. Remember, the more time you spend studying, the better your chances of achieving your goal of a passing score.

STUDYING FOR CSET: ENGLISH

It is very important for you to choose the time and place for studying that works best for you. Some students set aside a certain number of hours every morning to study, while some choose the night before going to sleep, and others study during the day, while waiting in line, or even while eating lunch. Choose a time when you can concentrate and your study will be most effective. Be consistent and use your time wisely. Work out a study routine and stick to it.

When you take a practice test, simulate the conditions of the actual test as closely as possible. Turn your television and radio off and sit down at a quiet table. When you complete the practice test, score it and thoroughly review the explanations to the questions you answered incorrectly. Do not, however, review too much at any one time. Concentrate on one problem area at a time by examining the question and explanation, and by studying our review until you are confident that you have mastered the material. Keep track of your scores to discover areas of general weakness and to gauge your progress. Give extra attention to the review sections that cover your areas of difficulty, as this will build your skills and confidence on test day.

ABOUT THE REVIEW SECTIONS

The subject review in this book is designed to help you sharpen the basic skills needed to approach the CSET: English test, as well as provide strategies for attacking the questions.

Each subtest is examined separately, clearly delineating the content domains. The skills required for all subtests fulfill the objectives of the CCTC and the Content Standards for California Public Schools and are extensively discussed to optimize your understanding of what each specific CSET: English subtest covers.

Your schooling has taught you most of what you need to succeed on the test. Our review is designed to help you fit the information you have acquired into each specific subtest content domain. Reviewing your class notes and textbooks together with our reviews will give you an excellent springboard for passing the test.

SCORING CSET: ENGLISH

Multiple-Choice Questions

A candidate's performance on CSET: English with multiple-choice questions is based strictly on the number of test questions answered correctly. Candidates do not lose any points for wrong answers. Each multiple-choice question counts the same toward the total score. These items are scored electronically and checked to verify accuracy.

Two Types of Constructed-Response Questions

Both extended-response and short-response constructed-response questions are focused responses that require a breadth of understanding of each subtest's content domain and the ability to relate concepts from different aspects of the field.

Extended-response questions take approximately 45–60 minutes to complete, whereas short-response questions take 10–15 minutes each to complete. Both will be scored by at least two qualified California educators using two sets of performance characteristics and two scoring scales.

Extended-response constructed-response questions: Scorers focus on the extent to which a response fulfills the following performance characteristics:

Purpose: addressing the constructed-response assignment in relation to relevant CSET subject matter and/or content specifications.

Subject Matter Knowledge: applying accurate subject matter knowledge as described in relevant CSET subject matter and/or content specifications.

Support: using appropriate, quality supporting evidence in relation to relevant CSET subject matter and/or content specifications.

Depth and Breadth of Understanding: the degree to which the response demonstrates understanding of the relevant CSET subject matter requirements.

Short-Response Questions: scorers focus on the same performance characteristics as the extended-response questions, omitting consideration for the Depth and Breadth of Understanding category.

You are given 5 hours to complete the test, so be aware of the amount of time you are spending on each question. Using the practice test will help you prepare to pace your time evenly, efficiently, and productively.

Scoring scales will be found at the end of Practice Test 1, Subtest III and Subtest IV.

SCORE RESULTS

After you have taken the CSET, you will receive a score report for your records. Your results will also be sent to the CCTC and any institutions you indicated when you registered.

For each subtest taken on the CSET: English, your score report will include your passing status and, if you did not pass, your total subtest score. The reverse side of the score report contains diagnostic information about your performance.

Each CSET subtest is scored separately and a passing score on each subtest is required to pass the examination. For each CSET subtest, an individual's performance is evaluated against an established standard. The passing score for each subtest was established by the CCTC based on the professional judgments and recommendations of California educators.

Passing status is determined on the basis of total subtest performance. The total subtest score is based on the number of raw score points earned on each section (multiple-choice section and/or constructed-response section), the weighting of each section, and the scaling of that score. Raw scores are converted to a scale of 100 to 300, with the scaled score of 220 representing the minimum passing score.

TEST-TAKING TIPS

Although some of you may not be familiar with tests like the CSET, this book will help acquaint you with this type of test and help alleviate your test-taking anxieties.

Tip 1. Become comfortable with the format of the CSET. When you are practicing, stay calm and pace yourself. After simulating the test only once, you will boost your chances of doing well, and you will be able to sit down for the actual test with much more confidence.

Tip 2. Read all of the possible answers. Just because you think you have found the correct response, do not automatically assume that it is the best answer. Read through each choice to be sure that you are not making a mistake by jumping to conclusions.

Tip 3. Use the process of elimination. Go through each answer to a question and eliminate as many of the answer choices as possible. By eliminating two answer choices, you have given yourself a better chance of getting the item correct since there will only be two choices left from which to make your guess. Try to answer all questions; you are not penalized for wrong answers, but you are rewarded for correct ones.

Tip 4. Place a question mark in your answer booklet next to answers you guessed, then recheck them later if you have time.

Tip 5. Work quickly and steadily. Avoid focusing on any one problem too long. Taking the practice tests in this book for your CSET test will help you learn to efficiently budget your time.

Tip 6. Learn the directions and format of the test. This will not only save time, but will also help you avoid anxiety (and the mistakes caused by getting anxious).

Tip 7. Be sure that the answer circle you are marking corresponds to the number of the question in the test booklet. The multiple-choice section is graded by machine and marking one answer in the wrong circle can throw off your answer key and your score. Be extremely careful.

THE DAY OF THE TEST

Before the Test

On the day of the test, make sure to dress comfortably, so that you are not distracted by being too hot or too cold while taking the test. Plan to arrive at the test center early. This will allow you to collect your thoughts and relax before the test, and will also spare you the anguish that comes with being late.

You should check your CSET Registration Bulletin and other registration information to find out what time to arrive at the testing center.

Before you leave for the test center, make sure that you have your admission ticket and the following identification:

- one piece of current, government-issued identification, in the name in which you registered, bearing your photograph and signature
- one clear and legible photocopy of your original government-issued identification for each test session in which you are testing (i.e., one copy for the morning and/or one copy for the afternoon session)
- one additional piece of identification (with or without a photograph)

Note: If you do not have the required identification, you will be required to complete additional paperwork and have your photograph taken. This additional step will result in a reduction of your available testing time.

You must bring several sharpened No. 2 pencils with erasers, as none will be provided at the test center.

If you would like, you may wear a watch to the test center. However, you may not wear one that has a calculator, or one that makes noise. Dictionaries, textbooks, notebooks, briefcases, laptop computers, packages, and cell phones will not be permitted. Drinking, smoking, and eating are prohibited.

During the Test

You are given 5 hours to complete the CSET. Restroom breaks are allowed, but they count as testing time. Procedures will be followed to maintain test security. Once you enter the test center, follow all of the rules and instructions given by the test supervisor. If you do not, you risk being dismissed from the test and having your scores cancelled.

When all of the materials have been distributed, the test instructor will give you directions for filling out your answer sheet. Fill out this sheet carefully since this information will be printed on your score report. Once the test begins, mark only one answer per question, completely erase unwanted answers and marks, and fill in answers darkly and neatly.

After the Test

When you finish your test, hand in your materials and you will be dismissed. Then, go home and relax—you deserve it!

CSET STUDY SCHEDULE

The following study schedule allows for thorough preparation to pass CSET: English. This is a suggested six-week course of study. This schedule can, however, be condensed if you have less time available to study, or expanded if you have more time. Whatever the length of your available study time, be sure to keep a structured schedule by setting aside ample time each day to study. Depending on your schedule, you may find it easier to study throughout the weekend. No matter which schedule works best for you, the more time you devote to studying, the more prepared and confident you will be on the day of the test.

Week	Activity
1	Read and study the Introduction, *Passing the CSET: English Test*. This chapter will introduce you to the format of the exam and give you an overview of the subtests on each English exam. Consult the website at *http://www.cset.nesinc.com* for any further information you may need.
2	Take the first practice test for each of the four subtests on CD-ROM. Use the answer key with explanations to identify your areas of strength and those areas where you need more study. Make a list of subject areas where you need additional aid.
3	Study the review section of this book, taking notes, particularly on the sections you need to study most. Writing will aid in your retention of information. Textbooks for college English will help in your preparation.
4	Review and condense your notes. Develop a structured outline detailing specific acts. It may be helpful to use index cards to aid yourself in memorizing important facts and concepts.
5	Take the second practice test for each of the four subtests on CD-ROM. Review the explanations for the questions you answered incorrectly.
6	Re-study any areas you consider to be difficult by using your study materials, references, and notes. If you need a final confidence boost, take the tests again in this book.

Chapter 1

Literature and Textual Analysis, and Composition and Rhetoric

Review for SMR Domain 1:

Literature and Textual Analysis,

Review for SMR Domain 3:

Composition and Rhetoric

Imagine I have a thousand random people who all say they want to be English instructors. They say things like "I like to read" and "I like to write my own poetry," but that doesn't tell me which ones would make the best educators. It doesn't answer the most important question of all, which is "Who is the person I'd like to have teaching my children?" Well, one way to determine the best candidates is to ask a series of generalized questions along with topic-specific questions to see who can not only give the right answers but who can also apply the knowledge they've acquired in a practical way. If I were judging candidates, I'd ask generalized survey-course-style questions such as "What is a common trait of epic poetry?" or "Why are orphans a common trope of Victorian literature?" I'd also ask a series of specific questions, such as "Who wrote *The Canterbury Tales*?" "What is the difference between a Shakespearean sonnet and an Italian sonnet?" and "When was Mary Shelley's *Frankenstein* first published?" That way I could determine which candidate is knowledgeable in a variety of areas across the curriculum. But telling someone the features of a Petrarchan sonnet, for example, is very different from recognizing one when two random sonnet samples are put side-by-side. And recognizing a Petrarchan sonnet is very different from writing one. So, not only would I want to see that candidates know the important components of English language and literature, but I'd also want to see them demonstrate their abilities in the application of that knowledge.

CSET Tip

Learn what the test is looking for.

Now you have an understanding of the CSET: English Test from the test's point of view. Maybe understanding what the test is looking for will make it appear less threatening.

PUTTING THE TEST IN PERSPECTIVE

As I said, the CSET is a way of verifying that you know enough about the basic principles of the English discipline to become an English educator. When you understand this rationale from the perspective of the test itself, you will more than likely find the test a lot less threatening. And having to demonstrate your knowledge makes sense, of course, because the person teaching you or your children should be someone who knows what they are talking about, right? Someone wishing to be an English teacher should know that a period goes at the end of a sentence, that a string of words must contain a noun (subject) and a verb (action) to be a complete sentence, that Homer's *Odyssey* is an *epic* poem, and that Geoffrey Chaucer wrote *The Canterbury Tales*. Think about it. Don't you expect the mechanic who works on your car to have a solid theoretical and practical understanding of the internal combustion engine? Wouldn't you want your doctor to know the theoretical and practical physiology of human anatomy before he or she performed surgery? Likewise, you must have a basic understanding of the theoretical and practical aspects of the English discipline before you can become an English teacher. And that's what the CSET asks you to demonstrate.

So the best way I can think to approach these section overviews, or walk-throughs, is to talk about them in terms of their unique fundamental elements and how to apply those unique fundamentals to the test. Because the test is looking for your understanding and your application of English fundamentals, I'll make some suggestions regarding practice techniques that ought to have you feeling well prepared come test time.

First, let's look at one familiar way to apply fundamentals during the actual test. Say for example that the test asks for the characteristics of an *epic*.

What are the characteristics of an *epic* poem?

(A) A story either in prose or verse, involving events, characters, and what those characters say and do

(B) Poems that use an ordinary speaking voice and a relaxed, almost satirical treatment of their subject matter

(C) A long narrative poem on a serious subject told in a formal and/or elevated style, centering on a heroic figure

(D) A long, usually depressing poem about heroes and mythic figures, and their relationship to the everyday world

While I might not be certain of the correct answer, I can figure it out by understanding the fundamental components of each genre and applying my knowledge to the test question and answers. I know that an epic is a long narrative poem, formal in style, that focuses on a specific, usually flat, heroic character and his heroic feats of bravery. In addition, the main character is usually a larger-than-life, semi-divine being (quasi-superhuman) who usually journeys on an extended quest (rather than simple wanderlust), during which quest the fate of his group or perhaps the fate of the entire world hangs in the balance. Now, reviewing the answer choices, I see that the answer that comes closest to my understanding of an epic is (C).

This same principle of deductive reasoning works conversely in that it will tell me which answer is *not* correct, as in the following example:

A single stanza lyric poem consisting of fourteen iambic pentameter lines, ending in a heroic couplet, is better known by what familiar literary term?

(A) Franciscan or Italian soliloquy

(B) Petrarchan or Shakespearean sonnet

(C) English or Anglo-Saxon elegy

(D) Homeric or Spenserian epistolary

At first, this seems like a tough question if you don't already know the answer. But here's what I do know: a *soliloquy* is a theatrical convention whereby a character, alone onstage, will talk to him- or herself or to the audience. So the answer cannot be (A), since a stage actor seldom has a "line limit" and is not required to speak in a certain poetic meter. An *elegy*, on the other hand, is a formal poem that laments the death of a particular individual and usually ends with some form of consolation or reconciliation on the part of the speaker. Since none of these concepts appear in the question, it's safe to presume that (C) is not an appropriate answer either. An *epistolary* is a style of prose fiction written in the form of letters and journal entries. So, that makes (D) incorrect. The only answer left is (B), a *sonnet*, which indeed must be fourteen iambic pentameter lines long just as it must end in a heroic couplet.

Knowing these stylistic differences allows me to read any test sample and if the sample's focus is lamenting (mourning) the loss of a loved one, I'll know it's most likely an *elegy*. If the test sample shows daring feats of bravery or extended movement on the part of the superhuman protagonist, than it is most likely an *epic*. If I encounter a sample with letters, diary excerpts, and journal entries, I already know it's an *epistolary format*, and so on.

A principle to remember for test success: to succeed in passing the CSET, you'll want to think in the most fundamental (basic) terms possible.

LITERATURE AND TEXTUAL ANALYSIS (SMR DOMAIN 1)

Including

Textual Analysis (SMR 1.1)

Literary Elements (SMR 1.2)

Literary Criticism (SMR 1.3)

Analysis of Non-Literary Texts (SMR 1.4)

Textual analysis (the dissecting of a literary work) is a form of critical thinking or close reading whereby you are able to "read between the lines" of a story, poem, play, historical document, or essay passage and understand, on some level, the author's implied (thematic) meaning. The Literary Analysis (SMR 1.1) subtest will require you to recognize, compare, and evaluate various literary traditions, including:

- American (inclusive of cultural pluralism)
- British (inclusive of cultural pluralism)
- World literature and literature in translation (inclusive of cross-cultural literature)
- Mythology and oral tradition

You will also need to refresh your knowledge of the most basic components—the fundamental literary elements (SMR 1.2)—that make up a story.

FUNDAMENTAL LITERARY ELEMENTS

plot: the action that takes place in a story

setting: the location where a story takes place (indoors or outdoors, city or country, Earth or Mars, etc.) and the time during which the action occurs (morning or evening, winter or summer, 1600 A.D. or 2600 B.C.E., etc.)

characters: the people, or other "actors," in a story (protagonist and antagonist, for example)

point of view: the perspective from which a story is told (first person, second person, third person; omniscient, limited omniscient, etc.)

language: the writing style and word choices the author uses to create the tone of the story (figurative language; formal, informal, vernacular; didactic, pragmatic, pejorative, etc.)

symbol: something that represents or suggests something else by reason of a relationship, association, convention, or accidental resemblance; especially: a visible sign of something abstract or invisible (i.e. the lion is a symbol of courage, the oak is a symbol of strength, and the railroad is a symbol of modernity)

theme: the main idea or message of the story

As important as these fundamental story components are, you should also polish your *paraphrasing* (restating in your own words what you think you heard, read, saw, etc.) and *summarizing* (writing a brief synopsis of a story or story section) skills. When you read an excerpt from a story, poem, play, historical document, or essay, you should be able to recognize the author's meaning (theme), write a paraphrase of your recognition, and then summarize your paraphrase. To practice this, grab a literary anthology, newspaper, magazine, whatever is handy, and flip it open to a random page, read a paragraph or two, and think about its thematic meaning. Write a summary of your thoughts and then paraphrase your summary or summarize your paraphrase. Practicing this technique a few minutes at a time, at various times during your day, will pay off in improved concentration and greater confidence when you enter the testing area.

CSET Tip

Practice, practice, practice for improved concentration and greater confidence.

Using literary anthologies that provide feedbacks on and interpretations of each story will allow you to check your work. After reading a story, write your ideas first, then compare them to the anthology's analysis. Try to justify and support your *thematic interpretation* (understanding of the author's/story's meaning) with a direct example (quotation) or two or three from the story or poem. As you are reading, repeatedly ask yourself questions about events taking place in the story or poem. For example, when a character gives another character a red rose, is he simply sharing the bounty of his garden, or does the action and the particular flower itself have some symbolic meaning? Is the author using figurative language or perhaps a certain setting or environment to create a mood or feeling? Is the author being sarcastic? Scribble down your observations as you read, and get into the habit of thinking and writing in specific literary terms. *Annotate* stories (add your own expository and explanatory notes) and do the the summary-paraphrasing exercise regularly. By the time you get to the CSET, your test answers will flow as easily as your scribble notes, the process of writing will seem a lot less formal, and the test itself, less intimidating.

Essentially then, textual analysis is a process of repeatedly asking the types of questions mentioned earlier until you find a logical and supportable (defendable, justifiable) answer. It's one way of dissecting a literary work in terms of separating literary content (*Fagan, Oliver, Bill, Nancy, Dodger*, et al.) from authorial style and content (Charles Dickens, Dickensian). So while the CSET will use a wide variety of samples from arbitrary literary sources, the *analytical fundamentals* (deductive and inductive reasoning) that you use will remain constant. Symbols will be symbols no matter if they appear in a short story, a poem, a play, a historical document, or an essay. A protagonist will evolve as a result of a story's conflict and the antagonist will supply that conflict, whether the characters appear in a screenplay, a novel, a poem, or a short story. A rainy sky or dreary day will most likely represent melancholy just as spring represents new blossoms and new beginnings whether it's on stage or in a poem, and so on. The key to test success is to be sure you have a firm grasp of basic principles, which you can then apply as needed.

If you are still feeling puzzled by what I'm suggesting, please take a few more minutes to consider it further, because the more you understand and practice the textual analysis process, the more relaxed and ready you'll be come test time.

Let's continue along this same line of thinking. While you will want to review which poet wrote "Sailing to Byzantium," and which poet "wandered lonely as a cloud," your test success depends more on your understanding the differences between a modernist poet (W. B. Yeats) and a romantic poet (William Wordsworth). In preparation for the test, you'll need to make sure that you know the fundamental components of modernist poetry and romantic poetry (along with the various other canonized poetic and literary conventions, figures, periods, etc.). In other words, the test is designed not only to assess your understanding of literary specifics such as whether you know that Robert Herrick meditated "Upon Julia's Clothes," John Donne called the "Busy old fool, unruly Sun," a "Saucy pedantic wretch," and Alfred Lord Tennyson beckoned "Maud" to "Come into the garden," but also to check your understanding of literary genres (SMR 1.2), significant literary movements (SMR 1.1), and literary criticism (SMR 1.3).

CSET Tip

If you practice with this book and with literary materials, you will have taken the test several times over.

Thus a *modernist* poet like W. B. Yeats will use classical Greco-Roman images such as the ancient Greek city of Byzantium, just as he will use intellectual fragments and questions rather than answers to poetically explore the human condition. A *romantic* poet like William Wordsworth, on the other hand, will contemplate images of nature and express his "spontaneous overflow of powerful feeling" in a more "common" vocabulary while he poetically ponders the human condition. Equipped with this understanding of these two distinct poetic styles, you can go into the test knowing that when you encounter a piece of literature that you aren't familiar with—and you will—you will have the tools necessary to make an educated guess that more than likely will be the right answer. If you spend time practicing with the tests in this book, as well as with newspapers, magazines, literature and composition anthologies, and so on, you'll already have taken the test, or at least its equivalent, several times over.

Concentrating on fundamentals will help with ideas of interpretation for literary criticism (SMR 1.3) as well, regardless of whether the sample question is a work of fiction or a non-literary text (SMR 1.4) such as an historical document. Like an onion, a well-crafted piece of literature is composed of many separate yet attached layers, and thinking in distinct, layered terms will assist you in your literary criticisms as well. Mary Shelley's *Frankenstein* is an excellent example of a multilayered text.

Ways to Use Layers of Text as Basis for Criticism

Criticism Based on Gender

You may for example, summarize the *novella* (a short novel, usually fifty to one hundred pages in length) *Frankenstein* from the perspective of *gender*. That is, Dr. Frankenstein, a man, successfully "creates life" (i.e., gives "birth") without the intervention of a woman. If this summation of the story seems appropriate to you, then you'd be a using a gender- or feminist-based interpretation, and subsequently you would look at the story only in terms of gender issues. You'd want to find gendered examples in the sample passage and make note of situations where perhaps Dr. Frankenstein swoons (nearly faints; stereotypically, a decidedly female attribute) or otherwise behaves in a feminine manner. Or you might paraphrase how the female characters function in the story and so on, as long as it pertains to gender and gendered issues.

Criticism Based on Theological Conflict

And yet, the same story can be summarized as a *theological* conflict between science and religion, considering Dr. Frankenstein uses science to usurp God's life-giving power, and consequently *plays God himself*. Now you'd look through the story for passages regarding scientific exploration and academia, as well as dialogues pertaining to theology. These examples might include the relationship and responsibilities that exist between creator and creation, or what it means to "play God." In other words you'll be looking only at theological and scientific symbols and language, and so on, and how they function in Frankenstein's epistolary story.

Cultural-Based Criticism

Or *Frankenstein* can be thought of *culturally*, suggesting that the story reinforces the social stereotypes of class, race, and gender (including the idea of looks as a reflection of "good" and "evil"). After all, Dr. Frankenstein is an upper-class white male, presumably pleasant looking, who has the time, money, facilities, and education to perform his experiments (the ugly creature). If you follow this interpretational path, you'd be using a cultural-based form of critical interpretation, and thus, you'd look exclusively for examples of *multicultural* relationships and hierarchy, along with social stereotypes reinforcing concepts of rich, pretty, and handsome equaling good and moral, while poor, ugly, and unattractive represents bad and immoral.

Historically-Based Criticism

If these avenues don't sound intriguing, you can look at the publication date of the original text (1818), and ask yourself what (historically) was going on in England around the turn of the nineteenth century. Perhaps the onset of the Industrial Revolution had begun, and if so, then perhaps some of the social concerns of the day are represented in the story. As massive machines and factories are being built to "augment" (replace?) the human labor force, would the idea of "building a person" as one would build a machine sound so far-fetched? And isn't "building a person" exactly what Dr. Frankenstein does? It might well have been a legitimate concern. Now you'd look for examples of industrialization anxieties in the book, perhaps the dehumanizing and humanizing elements. This avenue of literary criticism, whereby you view the text as a product of its historical period and environment, is known as *new historicism*.

Notice that some works of literature lend themselves to a specific interpretive format. While *Frankenstein* may have a variety of avenues to follow, Frederick Douglass's "An Appeal to Congress," for example, clearly demands a multicultural or new-historicist approach. With racially charged language such as "If black men have no rights in the eyes of white men, of course the whites can have none in the eyes of the blacks," the essay is most easily and obviously analyzed within a multicultural and/or historical framework. So by all means, keep yourself on the path of least resistance, and avoid the urge to apply, say, feminist criticism to an obviously historical document.

The brief summations I've provided for the *Frankenstein* story and the Douglass essay hopefully give you a brief understanding of literary theory, criticisms, and interpretive styles. At the same time, you may also notice the brief summaries themselves could be used as simple yet effective thesis statements (a topic and a claim) for a basic essay.

COMPOSITION AND RHETORIC (SMR DOMAIN 3)

Including

Written Composing Processes (Individual and Collaborative; SMR 3.1)

Rhetorical Features of Literary and Non-Literary Oral and Written Texts (SMR 3.2)

Rhetorical Effects of Grammatical Elements (SMR 3.3)

Conventions of Oral and Written Language (SMR 3.4)

Research Strategies (SMR 3.5)

One of the pitfalls to watch for in CSET's section 1 is that the test will "switch gears" without warning, going from asking you a series of analytical questions (SMR1.1) to asking you a series of compositional and rhetorical questions (SMR 3). The good news is that your approach to these latter questions will mirror that used for the analytical questions: you will once again demonstrate your understanding of basic principles—this time, of composition and rhetoric—and apply those elements in one form or another.

Compose, a verb, suggests the act of putting something together, whereas *composition*, a noun, refers to the actual essay or other end result of the composing process. Thus, the CSET will test your knowledge of the compositional components necessary to write an academic paper (prewriting, drafting, thesis development, writing, supporting, revising, and editing) along with the features of a finished essay (voice; emotional [pathos], logical [logos], or ethical [ethos] appeals; logical fallacies, etc.).

You may recall that the first step in the process of analyzing a composition is determining the **audience** and **purpose** (SMR 3.1). Some of the examples used for the CSET will be relatively self-evident, such as Frederick Douglass's congressional appeal. It's rather obvious (remember to always state the obvious) from the title alone who the target audience is—it's Congress. The purpose for Douglass's writing/oration may not be as obvious at first, as Douglass might be trying to enlighten, persuade, instigate, cajole, motivate, entertain, or insult Congress, just to name a few options. By closely looking at the oration itself, you can see that Douglass reveals his motives when he suggests that African-Americans have a "right to a participation in the production and operation of government" just as much as their white Western-European counterparts do. So Douglass's speech can be called a "persuasive argument based on a logical premise promoting civil rights."

Once you have an understanding of Douglass's audience and purpose, you can look at the rhetorical features of his speech (SMR 3.2). You can, for example, point out (or be on the lookout for) the *inductive* and *deductive reasoning* behind his *thesis*, along with the *claims* (arguments that an idea is true), *warrants* (justifiable reasons), *stasis* (the crux of the argument), *syllogisms* (a form of deductive reasoning), *analogies* (comparisons), *factual* (fact-based) and *statistical* (numeric-based) *evidence* (support) he uses, and so on. At the same time you can also make note of the rhetorical effects of the grammatical elements, conventions, and strategies (SMR 3.3, SMR 3.4, and SMR 3.5) he's using. These grammatical elements will include the orator's use of precise vocabulary and effective diction to construct and/or control the composition's *voice*, *tone*, *style*, and so forth. It will also include fundamental elements of grammar such as active and passive sentences, ambiguous and concrete language and/or ideas, expletives, clichés, idioms, colloquialisms, and the like.

Of course, you'll want to refresh your knowledge of compositional and rhetorical jargon. An example of compositional and rhetorical jargon would include Aristotelian language of effective argument, such as "syllogisms, enthymemes, logos, ethos, pathos, stasis, warrants," and so on.

CSET Tip

When you read anything at all: paraphrase it, summarize it!

You should also thumb through various anthologies, scholarly journals, newspapers, and magazines, looking for that jargon as you skim random essays and articles and noting their various compositional and rhetorical techniques and strategies as well. Don't forget to write down your observations in a paraphrased *and* summarized sentence or two. If you do this for several articles in a variety of magazines, you'll essentially be taking one practice test after another. An issue of a well written, popular magazine would be a great place to start for this exercise.

The bulk of your study time, however, should be spent reviewing the basics of the English language in terms of grammatical and syntactical structures. Several sections of the test will include questions on composition fundamentals. So remind yourself what a **double-plural noun** is (a noun with two possible plural forms) and look for examples in newspapers, magazines, and other sources. Curl up with a basic grammar book and review the following terms, among others:

BASIC GRAMMAR TERMS

regular verbs: verbs that form the past tense by adding the suffix *–ed*, as in *rest, rested*

irregular verbs: verbs that form the past tense by changing spelling, as in *bring, brought*

common nouns: a nonspecific or informal name of a person, place, or thing; for example, *holiday*

proper nouns: the always-capitalized name of a specific person, place, or thing; for example, *Christmas*

pronouns: words that take the place of nouns, such as *he, she, you, I, it,* etc.

gerunds: nouns formed out of a verb by adding *-ing*, as in *I like **swimming*** (The direct object *swimming*—a noun—is formed from the verb *swim*.)

Knowing these and other standard grammatical elements and how they function is important in this section of the test, so spend a few minutes every day not simply reviewing these terms but also looking for examples of them in newspapers, magazines, and your other everyday reading. Along with irregular and regular verbs, common and proper nouns, and gerunds, elements such as **morphemes** (the smallest element of a word that still has meaning, such as *cat* or *pin*) and **affixes** (suffixes like *-ing* and *-ed*, and prefixes like *un-* and *re-*) won't be as hard to find on the test if you've already spent time finding them elsewhere.

Also in your reading, note the use of **active** and **passive voice**. An active sentence puts the **subject** (the performer of the verb's action) before the **object** (the receiver of the verb's action), as in *Joe's car* [subject] *hit* [verb] *the tree* [object]. A passive sentence puts the object before the subject, as in: *The tree* [object] *was hit* [verb] *by Joe's car* [subject]. Get into the habit of watching for and labeling these and other compositional conventions as you go through your daily routine. In your own writing, the use of the active voice is preferable. It is often stronger, and more easily understood by the reader.

In addition, the CSET will test your knowledge of the spoken and written conventions (SMR 3.4) of the English language. Terms such as **preferred usage** and **conventions** refer to the fact that there are standardized or formulaic principles (conventions) required for an effective argument. These principles can run the gambit from the inclusion of a thesis (supported by convincing evidence, followed by a conclusion), to maintaining a formal writing tone, to avoiding contractions and colloquialisms, etc. These preferred conventions remain constant, while other, more malleable components such as grammar, syntax, etc., fluctuate or change from generation to generation. Simply put: *I ain't not need too be two worried about you with this already, which, is, because, you can recognize many standards of "english" when you seen them and wear you don't.* (I think my senior editor just swooned like Dr. Frankenstein.)

Because the fundamentals of grammar are so ingrained in us, mistakes in usage and conventions are easily recognizable. However, being able to put the right name to the infractions is just as important as being able to recognize them. So, to practice, reread (look, I just used a prefix, *re-*, on that verb *read*) the italicized sentence in the previous paragraph. Now, get a red pen and, step-by-step, take an inventory of each grammatical infraction, noting why it is wrong and how you'd go about fixing it. Someday soon you'll be grading your students' papers in this same fashion. Can you find the double-negative, *ain't not*, or the improper spelling of *two* when I meant *to* (or did I mean *too*)? Are there other homophone problems? Do my subjects and verbs agree in tense and number? Are my parallel structures appropriate? Is my punctuation correct? Are proper nouns capitalized? Tear apart the sentence in terms of its grammatical infractions until no problems remain. Make sure you can correctly label each trouble spot *and*, more important, know how you'd correct what is fundamentally wrong. It will take only a few practice sessions before you should begin feeling comfortable with the necessary jargon and conventions of this section, and once you're familiar and comfortable with the material, well, you ain't gonna have no troubles with the CSET.

Research strategies and proper citation formats (SMR 3.5) are seemingly always being updated to accommodate the latest technologies, so regrettably there is little else to do but familiarize yourself with the latest edition of a basic grammar guidebook, such as Diana Hacker's *The Bedford Handbook* (now in its seventh edition), and the Modern Language Association's latest *MLA Handbook for Writers of Research Papers*. The most recent editions of these style guides, and the multitude of alternate titles available, will offer you the time-honored basics along with the most technologically up-to-date conventions regarding proper paper and citation formats, research techniques, and mechanics. Although you most likely already own one or more of these invaluable guidebooks, make sure the editions you have are recent enough to include the current technology. If you don't own such a book or your style guide has a copyright date of 1923, now's the time to get a new one, because most contemporary handbooks not only include the most current information and documentation standards, but they also list links to free supplemental websites, which can be very helpful resources for extra information, extra practice, and instant feedback.

Ultimately, you want to avoid razzle-dazzle at all costs. You are *not* there to impress the CSET committee! Nothing you write will make them say, "Wow!" This "wow factor" stuff is a myth. You are taking the test to show the judges that you know enough to enter the discipline. That's it. Your sole purpose is to demonstrate that you have the abilities, skills, and understanding necessary to become an effective academic. So don't give in to the urge to write your dissertation on the essay sections. Avoid overwriting just as you'd avoid oversimplification. Concentrate on one clear topic at a time.

Understanding what the test is looking for is the best way to prepare for what's coming.

Chapter 2

Language, Linguistics & Literacy

Review for SMR Domain 2:

Language, Lunguistics & Literacy

HUMAN LANGUAGE STRUCTURES (SMR 2.1)

Including

    Acquisition and Development of Language and Literacy (SMR 2.2)

    Literacy Studies (SMR 2.3)

    Grammatical Structures of English (SMR 2.4)\

The second section of the CSET will ask you to demonstrate your knowledge regarding the linguistic aspects of English. The section will focus more on the scientific and physiological methodology of language rather than the aesthetic or philosophical aspects of language and literature.

In this section you'll be asked questions about:

morphology: the structure (or construction) of words

inflections: variations in pitch and tone

derivations: formation of words from root words, gerunds, affixes, and so forth

phonology: the sounds of language and the physiological production thereof

syntax: organizational structure of both words and sentences

etymology: the study of word origins and evolution

semantics: the meaning of words in a language.

To demonstrate your knowledge regarding human language structures (SMR 2.1), as opposed to whale, insect, Klingon, or primate language structures, you'll be asked if you know the syntactic differences among languages and the universalities of languages. The test will ask you about linguistic structures and whether you can recognize the nature of human language. This section will cover topics such as *pidgin languages* (a simple language comprised of elements of two or more independent languages, allowing people to communicate and negotiate when they speak different languages). *Wan-fela man* (meaning "one-fellow man") and *wan-pisi haws* (meaning "one-piece house") are examples of nineteenth-century Chinese-English pidgin expressions and their meanings; note the similarities and differences to our language.

When these pidgins transcend generations and become part of the indigenous language, they are known as **Creoles**. In Guyanese Creole, for example, *i-wiiri* translates to "he is weary," with the *i* pronounced as an *e* sound or if you prefer, with the *h* in *he* as a silent letter. So, *i-wok* doesn't refer to me stir-frying, it means "he works." French-English Creole works the same way in that the greeting *Bonjou, ti dam. Ki jan ou ye*? (Hello, ma'am. How are you?) and the response *M byen, wi* (I am fine) contain remnants of both their French and English origins, yet represent a hybrid of two distinct languages into one commonly discernable language.

You might think of *etymology* (the origin and history of words) as a bridge between the universality of languages and the familiarity of our own language, as English words are rooted in several other languages. The word *etymology* itself dates back to at least the Middle English period. Its origins are Latin, *etymologia*, and Greek, *etymología*. Along with the origin of words, etymology explores the evolution of word definitions over the course of their usage. Word definitions change over time, or adopt additional meanings, as in the case of the word *mouse*, which used to refer only to a small rodent. The word *passion* is another good example of how word meanings change over time. Derived from Old French, *passion* used to mean "Christ's suffering," but you may think of the word today as meaning "enthusiasm" or "excitement." And you don't need to be a linguist to know that the word *gay* does not mean today what it did when people donned *gay* apparel, so they could *deck the halls*.

It might help you to think, as many scholars do, of language as a "living entity" that evolves, develops, and grows over time. To vanquish this lexical behemoth you'll first want to remind yourself of basic linguistic and language fundamentals, like the evolution and functionality of words. Remember when *bad* used to function only as a negative? Today that same word can mean something very good, too. So start noticing words as they evolve: it's happening as we speak. Practice writing extended definitions of words and

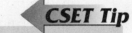

CSET Tip

Notice words as they evolve—it's happening all the time.

their ever-changing meanings. Then practically apply those words by finding them and using them in your daily routines. This practice will be of great value in getting you through the structural questions.

Language and Literacy

The Language and Literacy sections (SMR 2.2) will ask you to answer questions concerning language acquisition and development, that is, how we learn to speak as infants, or perhaps what influence our first language has on learning a second language. For example, in English, our adjectives usually appear before the noun they modify, such as in this sentence: *A mansion is a **big** house*. The adjective *big* appears before the noun *house*. However, this same sentence written in Spanish, *La mansión es una casa **grande***, places the adjective *grande* (big) after the noun it modifies, *casa* (house). Such variations in style and structure obviously have an impact on the learning of languages just as they will on the fundamentals of pronunciation. The *ch* sound in English, as in ***chew*** or ***chicken***, poses challenges for native Spanish-speaking individuals, because the same letter combination in Spanish is pronounced like the English *sh*, as in ***show*** or ***should***. Knowing these variations in language development helps to understand the derivations in speech patterns from one language to another. But it is rather unrealistic to ask you to learn every language in the world and each one's unique properties and idiosyncrasy by test day (or is it?).

The CSET doesn't expect you to know all of the world's languages. What it does expect is that you will know methods and techniques for acquiring and developing language and literacy skills, such as reading aloud to infants and preschoolers (which encourages, models, and develops cognitive thinking and overall literacy skills), *semantic mapping* (structuring linguistic information in a graph, chart, or map—what we used to call "sentence diagramming"), and *word analogies* (drawing a relationship between words or word groups, e.g., *girl/woman – boy/man*). and acquisition skills, such as the benefits of reading aloud to infants and preschoolers, which encourages, models, and develops cognitive thinking and overall literacy skills. This particular CSET section will present information based on test results and statistical information gathered from organizations such as the National Institute for Literacy (http://www.nifl.gov), the American Literacy Council (http://www.americanliteracy.com), the National Center for Family Literacy (http://www.famlit.org), the International Literacy Institute (http://www.literacy.org), and academic institutions known for their literacy programs and for their advocacy in solving the global crisis of illiteracy, such as Cornell University (http://cornell.edu). For example, according to the Los Angeles Public Library System, illiteracy costs the nation "more than $225 billion a year in lost productivity. It is tied to unemployment, crime, poverty, and family problems. For example, 75% of unemployed adults have reading and/or writing difficulties, 60% of all juvenile offenders have problems reading, while $5 billion is spent each year on welfare and unemployment compensation due to illiteracy."

Most literacy institutions and universities have helpful, user-friendly, informative websites that present essential elements and information. Purdue University's OWL Writing Lab, http://owl.english.purdue.edu; The University of Indianapolis Writing Lab, http://www.learningpt.org; and The Bedford Research Room, http://bedfordstmartins.com/researchroom; are good places to start. Much of the information is free and downloadable, so you can review the information more comfortably and at your own convenience. The materials (articles, charts, graphs, etc.) from these websites will also suggest that global illiteracy has in fact reached epidemic proportions, while offering numerous ways to solve the problem. Certainly a look at these Internet-based resources is a good place to start your section review, because the test will most likely include questions on language acquisition and literacy development for both children and adult learners.

Grammatical Structures of English

The Grammatical Structures of English section (SMR 2.4) is very close to the Conventions of Oral and Written Language section (SMR 3.4), so being well-prepared for one section will greatly increase your chances for success in the other. In this section you will be asked about the methods of sentence construction, including, but of course not limited to the following.

SENTENCE CONSTRUCTION

noun phrases: noun phrases include the noun and all its modifiers, as in *the big red bouncy **ball***

subordinate clauses: clauses that add additional information to a sentence but cannot stand alone as a sentence, as in *People **who live in glass houses** should not throw stones.*

verb complements: are direct or indirect objects of a verb. They may be nouns, pronouns, or words or word groups acting as nouns.

verb phrases: add when, where, why, and how information about the action as in, "she cut off her nose—the action—*to spite her face*" tells *why* she did it)

modals: or modal auxiliaries, are helping verbs. They are always accompanied by other verbs, never conjugated, and are followed by the simple form of the verb. Some examples are *can, could, may, might, must, must not,* and *should.*

count and **non-count nouns:** count nouns refer to things that can be counted; they have both a singular and plural form, the latter usually formed by adding an *s*: *dog, dogs*. Non-count nouns refer to things that cannot be counted; they are neither singular nor plural, but are treated as singular in a sentence. Some examples are *education, courage,* and *anger*.

prepositions: words such as *of, in, at, over, under, below, near,* and *against* that indicate the relationship of one thing to another

---

For this section I recommend the same study techniques as I did for section 3.4 on page 15. First, with a basic grammar guide like *The Bedford Handbook*, refresh yourself on the jargon, noting subtle differences between various types of noun and verbal phrases, sentence-embedding clausal and phrasal modifiers, and so forth. Next, thumb through various anthologies, scholarly journals, local and national newspapers, and various magazines, and skim over various and random prose, poetry, essays, and articles, looking at and noting their various grammatical structures, techniques, and mechanics. Map out several sentences at a time from diverse sources; mark noun phrases in local newspaper articles and verb phrases in national newspaper articles. Underline all the prepositions in an issue of *People*, *Time*, or *Newsweek*, and circle all the adverbs the next day. Read an article in a *Harper's* magazine, and note how the adjectives are used. Know the grammatical jargon *and* how each component functions in everyday situations—TV, newspapers, magazines, and the like—so that when you enter the testing room, you'll feel comfortable recognizing the various grammatical structures regardless of the sources from which they have come. In essence, you'll be taking a practice test each time you mark up an article, and the more practice tests you take, the easier the real one will seem.

Chapter 3

Communications: Speech, Media, and Creative Performance

Review for SMR Domain 4:

Communications: Speech, Media, and Creative Performance

3

ORAL COMMUNICATION PROCESSES (SMR 4.1)

Including

Media Analysis and Journalistic Applications (SMR 4.2)

Dramatic Performance (SMR 4.3)

Creative Writing (SMR 4.4)

The exchange of information between individuals, for example, by means of speaking, writing, or using a common system of signs or behavior: the act of communicating; the communication of information.

Communication, as defined in the Encarta Online Dictionary

While most universities segregate the English department from the Communications department before they separate those departments into subdivisions such as journalism, creative writing, theater arts, and so on, the CSET puts them all back together again under the blanket of English. So, many English-major test takers are likely to find the topics covered in this section or parts of this section unfamiliar or intimidating.

That being said, the generic principles that pertain to the rest of the test sections, understanding principle elements and being able to recognize, label, and apply those elements, become even more relevant here. That's because doing well on this section isn't so much about knowing the topics themselves as it is about demonstrating your ability to write an effective essay on various topics. While the topics may seem a bit unfamiliar to you at first, the principles of essay writing are hopefully already familiar and habitual for you. Once you've read through this chapter and understood and practiced applying the basic principles of *Oral Communication* (public speaking, SMR 4.1), *Media Analysis* (TV, radio, Internet) and *Journalistic Applications* (newspapers, TV news, magazines; SMR 4.2), *Dramatic Performances* (theater, SMR 4.3), and *Creative Writing* (SMR 4.4), these principles should be familiar enough to you that all you'll need to concentrate on is the writing of a clean, clear, expository essay. More on the essay process in a moment. First, let me tell you about my personal test-prep experience.

Media Analysis and Journalistic Applications

My degrees are in the field of English literature, which means as a student, I had very little exposure to the theater arts, oral communications, or journalism departments except as a patron. Then I realized two things. One was that, although I hadn't had any courses such as Directing 101, Fundamentals of Public Speaking, or Cub Reporter 055, I had read and researched a ton of newspaper articles, journal articles, essays, and so forth. I watched way too much TV (media), listened to the radio, viewed billboards, and I'd attended live performances, both on and off campus. I began to ask myself what made some of these shows (or advertisements, or articles, etc.) more memorable (effective) than others. I checked out basic, Intro-101-type books on drama (journalism, public speaking, and creative writing) from the local community college library and thumbed through them, becoming familiar with the jargon and the fundamental components that go into the production of a play, for example. I prepared just as I would for a literary analysis. First, I brainstormed a rough outline of the essential components required for staging a theatrical production, such as lighting, sound, staging/blocking, actors, sets, and so forth. I say *required* because I focused only on the elements that are needed for a successful production and avoided distraction—well, mostly avoided distraction with theatrical sundries, since you can have a show without a curtain, but not without an actor. Once I had this outline roughed out, I found it relatively easy to go back and think of the productions I'd seen in terms of their individual components. I realized that the memorable productions were memorable precisely because they were successful in the same individual areas I had outlined. In each instance, I'd heard the actors clearly, not because of my seat location, but because the performers were *projecting* their voices, while at the same time they *enunciated* clearly, making their words both heard and understood from anywhere in the theater. I considered my view of the stage, again not in terms of seat location, but in terms of the actors' movements and how they were *blocked* out by the director. No one person obstructed or upstaged another. I considered the *set designs* and realized they too had been laid out so that they enhanced each scene, rather than obstructing, distracting, or overpowering it. The *stage lighting* was complementary to the performers and appropriate to the mood of the scene, no "disco balls in *Macbeth*" kind of stuff.

Perhaps you are getting the same idea I did. When I thought about the audience responses I'd already written, about the shows I'd seen and analyzed, and the books I'd reviewed, I realized I inherently knew more about the theater than I thought I did, and essentially I had already taken a practice test each time I'd analyzed a production of a movie, a play, or a TV show. Because I'd already mapped out several outlines of basic directorial components and had already become familiar with the basic theatrical terminology, the test question(s) and the language used seemed remarkably non-threatening. From that point on, I was able to relax and concentrate my efforts toward writing a solid (basic) expository essay. Of course, I had to repeat the process with speech, journalism, and creative writing, spending the most study time with the topics with which I was least familiar.

My second helpful realization was the understanding that as a literature major, I'd analyzed many plays, stories, and other works. So it was easy for me to think of live theater productions in terms of an extension of the directorial and production notes that annotate many plays printed in book form. This time I thumbed through various editions of various play genres, written by various authors of various nations, at various time periods throughout history, and focused my attention on the directorial and production notes rather than the dialogue. I connected with the actual performance text only enough to get a sense of what was supposed to be happening on the stage, that is, were the characters supposed to be happy or sad or angry or falling in love? I visualized which characters where supposed to be saying what to whom, and why, what their moods and actions were, and so on. I returned to my rough outline and added more notes.

Basic theater, journalism, mass media, public speaking, and creative writing books will give you the generic information that you'll need to know to get you through this section of the test. But remember, it's also *the application of the information* that the CSET wants to see from you. So spend a modest amount of time looking at and making notes about TV dramas, comedies, and commercials in terms of their directorial and production elements and techniques. Did I just recommend watching TV as a form of test preparation?

The reason for this practice application time seems evident enough. It's one thing to say, "A verb is an action word," or "An effective public speaker maintains eye contact with the audience," but does that mean you can underline all the verbs on the front page of today's newspaper or explain the intrinsic value of eye contact to a public speaker? Spend as much or more time *applying* the precepts you're reviewing as you do reviewing itself. Knowing that an effective thesis is made up of a topic and a claim is a very different experience from having to write an effective thesis. As a consumer of journalism and media, you already have a working knowledge of audience (you) and demographics (yours), so use this knowledge to your advantage when answering the questions, but before test day, make sure to practice applying the knowledge in the safety and comfort of your own home. You can review your own work so you'll see immediately which areas are your strengths and which subjects require more attention. Begin watching TV commercials and programs with a critical eye, and make notes as you watch: notes that recognize, label, and evaluate the media strategies, elements, and techniques involved. Check your comments against the information in the intro books. Thus, you can prepare for the media, journalism, and dramatic performance sections in the much same way as you do for the grammar sections.

Creative Writing, Composition & Rhetoric

As I said earlier in this walk-through, the most important thing to remember about the essay section is the essay itself. Don't let yourself get sidetracked or distracted by the topic. Don't struggle with ideas beyond your understanding of public speaking, for example. If a question were to ask, "Why is maintaining eye contact with your audience such an important component of an effective oral presentation?" think simply and specifically in terms of what

CSET Tip

Don't get sidetracked by the topic.

someone making eye contact means to *you*. Perhaps eye contact suggests a more honest or more caring intent on the part of the speaker, or perhaps it shows that the speaker is talking *to* you rather than *at* you. That's good enough! Stop thinking and start writing a clean, clear, and complete expository (detailed description discussing a topic's meaning or implications) essay that explains how eye contact shows a speaker's integrity. If the CSET question asks for two ways eye contact is effective, you already have the second idea down, so repeat the explanatory process showing how eye contact makes the listener feel involved. Don't think past the benefits of eye contact that you've already noted and don't change your topic or voice in midstream. Instead, think concrete language, paraphrase, summary, supporting evidence, and other compositional basics because *this is an expository essay section*. Stay focused on your writing skills such as a brief opening and clear thesis statement (topic: *direct eye contact*; claim: *shows a speaker's integrity*) based on a logical premise. Follow the thesis with a body (a paragraph or two) of supporting evidence (quotations, facts, or examples taken from any test samples, if available) and a conclusion that reiterates your original thesis statement. Don't allow yourself to forget that you are demonstrating your writing and thinking skills; concentrate on being pragmatic and didactic as you write with brevity, objectivity, and clarity.

CSET Tip

Write with brevity, objectivity, and clarity.

Remember, the CSET and a plethora of nationwide tests just like it are rites of passage we all must go through if we want to enter the discipline. But there is a light at the end of the tunnel. You can succeed. Having gone through the anxiety that accompanies such academic milestones, I can tell you that it *is* a long and arduous day of testing. Yet, after all is said and done and the test is behind you, you'll realize that if it had been easy, everyone would have done it. And that is precisely what makes all your time and effort so very worthwhile.

All the best.

Practice Test 1

Subtest I –
Literature and Textual Analysis;
Composition and Rhetoric

This practice test is also on CD-ROM in our special interactive CSET: English TEST*ware*®. It is highly recommended that you first take this exam on computer. You will then have the additional study features and benefits of enforced timed conditions and instant, accurate scoring. See page xvii for instructions on how to get the most out of REA's TEST*ware*®.

Practice Exam 1, Subtest I
Answer Sheet

1. Ⓐ Ⓑ Ⓒ Ⓓ
2. Ⓐ Ⓑ Ⓒ Ⓓ
3. Ⓐ Ⓑ Ⓒ Ⓓ
4. Ⓐ Ⓑ Ⓒ Ⓓ
5. Ⓐ Ⓑ Ⓒ Ⓓ
6. Ⓐ Ⓑ Ⓒ Ⓓ
7. Ⓐ Ⓑ Ⓒ Ⓓ
8. Ⓐ Ⓑ Ⓒ Ⓓ
9. Ⓐ Ⓑ Ⓒ Ⓓ
10. Ⓐ Ⓑ Ⓒ Ⓓ
11. Ⓐ Ⓑ Ⓒ Ⓓ
12. Ⓐ Ⓑ Ⓒ Ⓓ
13. Ⓐ Ⓑ Ⓒ Ⓓ
14. Ⓐ Ⓑ Ⓒ Ⓓ
15. Ⓐ Ⓑ Ⓒ Ⓓ
16. Ⓐ Ⓑ Ⓒ Ⓓ
17. Ⓐ Ⓑ Ⓒ Ⓓ
18. Ⓐ Ⓑ Ⓒ Ⓓ
19. Ⓐ Ⓑ Ⓒ Ⓓ
20. Ⓐ Ⓑ Ⓒ Ⓓ
21. Ⓐ Ⓑ Ⓒ Ⓓ
22. Ⓐ Ⓑ Ⓒ Ⓓ
23. Ⓐ Ⓑ Ⓒ Ⓓ
24. Ⓐ Ⓑ Ⓒ Ⓓ
25. Ⓐ Ⓑ Ⓒ Ⓓ

26. Ⓐ Ⓑ Ⓒ Ⓓ
27. Ⓐ Ⓑ Ⓒ Ⓓ
28. Ⓐ Ⓑ Ⓒ Ⓓ
29. Ⓐ Ⓑ Ⓒ Ⓓ
30. Ⓐ Ⓑ Ⓒ Ⓓ
31. Ⓐ Ⓑ Ⓒ Ⓓ
32. Ⓐ Ⓑ Ⓒ Ⓓ
33. Ⓐ Ⓑ Ⓒ Ⓓ
34. Ⓐ Ⓑ Ⓒ Ⓓ
35. Ⓐ Ⓑ Ⓒ Ⓓ
36. Ⓐ Ⓑ Ⓒ Ⓓ
37. Ⓐ Ⓑ Ⓒ Ⓓ
38. Ⓐ Ⓑ Ⓒ Ⓓ
39. Ⓐ Ⓑ Ⓒ Ⓓ
40. Ⓐ Ⓑ Ⓒ Ⓓ
41. Ⓐ Ⓑ Ⓒ Ⓓ
42. Ⓐ Ⓑ Ⓒ Ⓓ
43. Ⓐ Ⓑ Ⓒ Ⓓ
44. Ⓐ Ⓑ Ⓒ Ⓓ
45. Ⓐ Ⓑ Ⓒ Ⓓ
46. Ⓐ Ⓑ Ⓒ Ⓓ
47. Ⓐ Ⓑ Ⓒ Ⓓ
48. Ⓐ Ⓑ Ⓒ Ⓓ
49. Ⓐ Ⓑ Ⓒ Ⓓ
50. Ⓐ Ⓑ Ⓒ Ⓓ

Literature and Textual Analysis; Composition and Rhetoric

Read the following stanza from Samuel Taylor Coleridge's poem "*The Rime of the Ancient Mariner*" then answer questions 1 through 3.

> Water, Water, every where
> And all the boards did shrink;
> Water, Water, ever where
> Nor any drop to drink.
> Coleridge, *Rime of...* lines 120 – 23
> (Project Gutenberg)

1. Coleridge's repeated references to "Water" suggest he is really talking about

   (A) the fact that he is very thirsty.

   (B) the fact that while 2/3 of the earth is covered in water, not all that water is meant for human consumption.

   (C) the water as a symbolic representation.

   (D) words that rhyme.

2. What might an icon such as (oceans of) water represent?

   (A) A massive, damp, cold, and dreary element

   (B) A gigantic, rough, inhospitable, alien environment

   (C) A beautiful, recreational, global, environment

   (D) An abundant, life-giving element

3. What does Coleridge suggest by his juxtaposing images of abundant water supplies with the Mariner's inability to consume that water?

    (A) That nourishing and / or life-giving elements surround us, but we are not always able or willing to access it

    (B) That the ocean is a big, violent, yet indifferent adversary

    (C) That the ocean can either be used by people for fun, nourishment, and recreation or destroyed by pollution, over-fishing, and global-warming

    (D) That the human body can be metaphorically connecting with the ocean

4. Romantic poets feel that isolation and alienation are important components to the creation of their poetry. What does alienation have to do with Romantic ideology?

    (A) Romantic poets feel isolated and alone.

    (B) To commune with nature, one needs to be alone with nature.

    (C) Romantic poets feel like aliens in their own country.

    (D) Romantic poets feel frustration over foreigners trying to take over their homeland.

5. According to William Wordsworth, Romantic poets create poetry based upon "the spontaneous overflow of powerful feelings." How can the Romantics claim to be "spontaneous" when poems such as "Lines Composed a Few Miles Above Tintern Abbey" are obviously crafted with diligence, patience, and meticulous attention to details?

    (A) Spontaneity is just a state of mind.

    (B) The inspiration of the poem is based on spontaneity, while the actual crafting of the poem is a work of art.

    (C) Romantics call themselves spontaneous in order to sound more sophisticated and eloquent than they really are.

    (D) Absorbing oneself in nature requires impulsive and spontaneous actions.

6. While impressionism is generally associated with painters such as Monet and Degas, authors such as Stephen Crane adapted the artistic techniques for their writings. Which statement would most accurately represent an impressionistic style of writing by an author such as Stephen Crane?

    (A) Colors play the most important role in a story's construction.

    (B) Human pain and suffering provide an effective base for a story's composition.

    (C) Life is a series of unpredictable and usually depressing events.

    (D) Environment is significant in determining human fate.

7. Hamlin Garlin and Bret Harte used realism to create texts. *Realism* is best defined as

    (A) the literary technique of realistically representing the nature of life and the social world, as it would appear to the common reader.

    (B) an attempt to subject passive representation to the impressions of natural, monolithic, and flagrant social designs and structures.

    (C) the representation of the human condition based on loose and free-flowing designs, pattern, and shapes.

    (D) the belief that human beings exist entirely in the order of nature and do not have a soul nor any participation in a religious or spiritual world beyond nature.

8. Another, more popular name for regional writing is

    (A) nationalism consciousness.
    (B) patriotism.
    (C) social conservatism.
    (D) local color.

9. What are the characteristics of an epic poem?

(A) A story either in prose or verse, involving events, characters, and what those characters say and do

(B) Poems that use an ordinary speaking voice and a relaxed, almost satirical treatment of their subject matter

(C) A long narrative poem on a serious subject told in a formal and/or elevated style, centering on an heroic figure

(D) A long, usually depressing poem about heroes and mythic figures, and their relationship to the everyday world

Read the following excerpt from Franz Kafka's "A Hunger Artist," then answer questions 10 and 11.

During these last decades the interest in professional fasting has markedly diminished. It used to pay very well to stage such great performances under one's own management, but today that is quite impossible. We live in a different world now. At one time the whole town took a lively interest in the hunger artist; from day to day of his fast the excitement mounted; everybody wanted to see him at least once a day; there were people who bought season tickets for the last few days and sat from morning till night in front of his small barred cage; even in the nighttime there were visiting hours, when the whole effect was heightened with torch flames; on fine days the cage was set out in the open air, and then it was the children's special treat to see the hunger artist; for their elders he was often just a joke that happened to be in fashion, but the children stood open-mouthed, holding each other's hands for greater security, marveling at him as he sat there pallid in black tights, with his ribs sticking out so prominently, not even on a seat but down among the straw on the ground, sometimes giving a courteous nod, answering questions with a constrained smile, or perhaps stretching an arm through the bars so that one might feel how thin it was, and then again withdrawing deep into himself, paying no attention to anyone or anything, not even to the all-important striking of the clock that was the only piece of furniture in his cage, but merely staring into vacancy with half shut eyes, now and then taking a sip from a tiny glass of water to moisten his lips.

10. In this paragraph, Kafka is using hunger as a metaphor for

(A) oil, watercolor, and acrylic paints.

(B) organized religion and spirituality.

(C) nothing; he's talking about food.

(D) social courtesy and social propriety.

11. What do "grown-ups" often think of the Hunger Artist?

(A) That he is merely a joke

(B) That he is quality entertainment

(C) That he is a sensitive artist

(D) That he is lonely and confused

12. An heroic couplet consists of lines of iambic pentameter that rhyme in pairs: *aa*, *bb*, *cc*, and so on. Who is credited with the introduction of this poetic style?

(A) Homer

(B) William Shakespeare

(C) Sophocles

(D) Geoffrey Chaucer

13. A sonnet, whether Italian or English, is

(A) a lyric poem consisting of a single stanza of fourteen lines of iambic pentameter linked by an intricate rhyme scheme.

(B) a lyric poem consisting of two stanzas of twelve lines of trochaic meter linked by an intricate rhyme scheme.

(C) an epic poem consisting of fourteen lines of iambic pentameter linked by a free-flowing rhyme scheme.

(D) A romantic poem consisting of a single stanza of fifteen lines of iambic pentameter linked by an intricate rhyme scheme that ends in an heroic couplet.

14. A soliloquy is

    (A) an extended medieval poem that follows a standardized *abab* rhyme scheme whereby an actor reflects on the existence of God.

    (B) a monologue in which an actor speaks his or her thoughts and feelings aloud.

    (C) a monologue in which an actor confesses his or her innermost feelings to the person whom he or she loves.

    (D) an extended dialogue between two principal actors, usually consisting of witty conversation and word play.

15. Who is the author attributed with writing *The Iliad* and *The Odyssey*?

    (A) Sophocles
    (B) Euclid
    (C) Homer
    (D) Ulysses

16. The art of transmitting culture, beliefs, heritage, mythologies, and so on, either in the form of prose and verse, by word of mouth is also known as

    (A) lyrical ballads.
    (B) romantic tradition.
    (C) cultural renaissance.
    (D) oral tradition.

17. John Donne is considered by many to be the archetype of the

    (A) Cavalier poets.
    (B) Graveyard school of poets.
    (C) pre-Raphaelite poets.
    (D) Metaphysical poets.

18. The rhetorical technique of appealing to a reader's sense of emotions is also known as

    (A) logos.

    (B) pathos.

    (C) ethos.

    (D) topos.

19. In the construction of an effective persuasive argument, you must include

    (A) a detailed explanation of your personal feelings and emotions as they pertain to the subject matter.

    (B) a detailed analysis of the social, literary, and historical contexts upon which the argument is based.

    (C) a full recognition and clear analysis of the counterargument showing its strengths and weaknesses.

    (D) an oversimplification of the opposing argument, which thereby demonstrates the absurdity of the opposition's point of view.

20. Which of the following examples is *not* considered a logical fallacy?

    (A) Paraphrasing

    (B) Non sequitur

    (C) Post hoc

    (D) Stereotypes

21. A short narrative of an interesting, amusing, or biographical incident that serves to elucidate a point or idea is also known as

    (A) a protagonist.

    (B) an onomatopoeia.

    (C) an anecdote.

    (D) a fiction.

Read the following paragraph from Frederick Douglass's essay "An Appeal to Congress for Impartial Suffrage," then answer questions 22 and 23.

A VERY limited statement of the argument for impartial suffrage, and for including the negro in the body politic, would require more space than can be reasonably asked here. It is supported by reasons as broad as the nature of man, and as numerous as the wants of society. Man is the only government-making animal in the world. His right to a participation in the production and operation of government is an inference from his nature, as direct and self-evident as is his right to acquire property or education. It is no less a crime against the manhood of a man, to declare that he shall not share in the making and directing of the government under which he lives, than to say that he shall not acquire property and education. The fundamental and unanswerable argument in favor of the enfranchisement of the negro is found in the undisputed fact of his manhood. He is a man, and by every fact and argument by which any man can sustain his right to vote, the negro can sustain his right equally. It is plain that, if the right belongs to any, it belongs to all. The doctrine that some men have no rights that others are bound to respect, is a doctrine which we must banish as we have banished slavery, from which it emanated. If black men have no rights in the eyes of white men, of course the whites can have none in the eyes of the blacks. The result is a war of races, and the annihilation of all proper human relations.

22. What is the most accurate paraphrase of Douglass's thesis?

   (A) "Limited statements of argument" are the most effective way to communicate with branches of government.

   (B) Since "man is the only government-making animal in the world", then it "is no less a crime that he shall acquire property or education."

   (C) "If black men have no rights," then only a "war of [the] races" will solve the problems of inequality.

   (D) "If the right [of equality] belongs to any, it belongs to all."

23. What does *enfranchisement* mean?

    (A) To allow the political privileges of operation and ownership or the license granted to an individual or group to market a company's goods or services in a particular territory

    (B) To grant the political privileges of citizenship, especially the right to vote

    (C) To grant the right of membership into a professional organization, that is, having such rights of membership

    (D) To allow the political freedom and privileges of sincere and honest personal expression

24. What American author is famous for such works as *Life on the Mississippi*, and *Innocents Abroad: or The New Pilgrim's Progress*?

    (A) Ambrose Bierce
    (B) Stephen Crane
    (C) Edgar Allan Poe
    (D) Mark Twain

25. Which American author began his writing career as a newspaper journalist?

    (A) Thomas Paine
    (B) Frederick Douglass
    (C) Ambrose Bierce
    (D) N. Scott Momaday

26. A syllogism consists of a

    (A) minor premise, a deduction, and a conclusion.
    (B) major premise, a minor premise, and an induction.
    (C) major induction, a minor premise, and a conclusion.
    (D) major premise, a minor premise, and a conclusion.

27. A rhetorical argument using deductive reasoning

    (A) builds from accepted truths to specific conclusions.

    (B) builds from specific conclusions to a larger premise.

    (C) builds from one minor premise to another.

    (D) builds from one specific conclusion to another.

28. According to Aristotelian logic, the use of narrative is

    (A) an effective form of argument that "should not be considered innocent moments of entertainment in political communication."

    (B) an ineffective form of argument that "should be considered innocent moments of entertainment in political communication."

    (C) an effective form of political argument "only by those who have nothing substantial or intelligent to base their premise upon."

    (D) an effective form of entertainment, but a distracting component of logical argument, and therefore, "should be left for the writers of fiction and poetry."

29. Which of the following examples would be considered an argument based upon logos?

    (A) Politicians want to hurt the elderly by cutting Medicare, and as the elderly have given us so much already, we must care for them in return. Therefore, we must raise taxes to support Medicare and thus provide for better geriatric services and care facilities.

(B) I am a good wife, a loving mother, and dedicated employee. I've been happily married for eighteen years, and I've been a dental technician for twenty-five years. My colleagues, family, and friends say I'm a hard worker. Therefore, I deserve your vote for mayor.

(C) We do not have enough money to pay for improvements to our transit system. And without such civic improvements, this transportation system will weaken and thus hinder our economy. Therefore, we should raise taxes to pay for a better transit system.

(D) The city's infrastructure is deteriorating at an alarming rate. Roads, sewers, communications, and the like are all in need of serious repairs and/or upgrades. What if you had an emergency and 911 was no longer available? Therefore, we must increase taxes to pay for the necessary improvements to our infrastructure, or you could be next.

30. A metaphor is an example of

(A) literal interpretation.
(B) figurative language.
(C) logical fallacies.
(D) somnambulism.

31. T. S. Eliot's *The Waste Land* is a poetic example of

(A) modernism.
(B) lyricism.
(C) ballads.
(D) an epic.

32. Stream of consciousness is a narrative method whereby

    (A) the literal term for one thing is applied to another (usually something with which it is closely associated), because of contiguity in common experience or social consciousness.

    (B) long passages of introspection, sense perceptions, conscious and half-conscious thoughts, memories, expectations, feelings, and random associations, describing in detail what passes through a character's awareness.

    (C) a descriptive, salient, or picturesque phrase is used in place of the ordinary name for something. It is most prevalent in Anglo-Saxon poetry.

    (D) figures of speech establish a striking parallel, usually an elaborate parallel, between two very dissimilar things or situations.

33. New historicism is a form of literary theory whereby

    (A) critics focus primarily on the response that the literature has produced and produces in perceptive readers.

    (B) critics focus primarily on the aesthetic representations of the historical period in which the literature was produced.

    (C) critics focus primarily on the attempt to position writings from earlier eras into modern conceptions and social ideologies.

    (D) critics focus primarily on the historical and cultural conditions under which the literature was produced.

Read the following Phillis Wheatley poem, then answer questions 34 and 35.

"On Being Brought from Africa to America"

'TWAS mercy brought me from my Pagan land,
Taught my benighted soul to understand
That there's a God, that there's a Savior too:
Once I redemption neither fought nor knew,
Some view our sable race with scornful eye,
"Their color is a diabolic die."
Remember, Christians, Negroes, black as Cain,
May be 'refined, and join the' angelic train.

34. What is the overall tone of the poem?

    (A)   Angry and resentful

    (B)   Frustrated and contemptuous

    (C)   Grateful and ironic

    (D)   Loving and faithful

35. The poem is written in

    (A)   couplets.

    (B)   enjambments.

    (C)   meters.

    (D)   stanzas.

36. Postcolonial literatures are

    (A)   antebellum literatures that heighten or intensify the experience of subjugated peoples, to provide a modern reader an understanding of the values and principles of the American colonial experience.

    (B)   works that study the interactions between European nations and the societies they colonized in the modern period. It often involves the political, social, and cultural independence of peoples formerly subjugated in colonial empires.

    (C)   a style of writing whose stories are characterized by grotesque, macabre, or fantastic characters and incidents in order to explore social issues and reveal the cultural temperament of the American South.

    (D)   a reflection of the social and cultural ideologies of the concurring peoples in order to understand and justify their motivations for their barbaric actions.

37. Some scholars contend that Miguel de Cervantes originally intended *Don Quixote* to be "little more than a parody of the popular romantic/chivalric novels of his time." What is a parody?

    (A) A literary work holding up human vices and follies to ridicule and scorn, in order to expose or discredit those same social vices and follies

    (B) A short fictitious story that illustrates a moral attitude or religious precept

    (C) A series or exchange of clever or amusing verbal retorts

    (D) A literary or artistic work in which the style of a serious author or piece is closely imitated for comedic effect or ridicule

38. What is a topic sentence?

    (A) A sentence usually located at the end of a paper that summarizes or concludes the essay

    (B) A sentence usually located at the beginning of a paper that follows the rhetorical principles established by Aristotle.

    (C) A sentence usually located at the beginning of a paper that states the main premise of the essay.

    (D) A sentence usually repeated throughout a paper that reiterates the social or political importance of the essay.

39. An epistolary novel is

    (A) the oldest form of prose fiction. These extended narratives came into being during the late Middle Ages.

    (B) an extended fictional narrative, written in the form of letters, diaries, and journal entries.

    (C) an extended fictional narrative in which an heroic figure embarks on a quest or other perilous journey.

    (D) an extended fictional narrative, usually dealing with fantasy and the supernatural.

40. A prominent convention in metaphysical poetry is the paradox. A paradox is a

    (A) statement or idea that on the surface seems to be self-contradicting or absurd, yet turns out to make sense or reflect a truth.

    (B) romantic representation of rural life and labors, usually involving images of peace and simplicity in country life.

    (C) speechless performance in which actors use only posture, gesture, bodily movements, and exaggerated facial expressions.

    (D) work of fiction containing supernatural events and situations that are not scientifically explainable.

41. Many modern poets, such as Emily Dickinson, W. B. Yeats, William Blake, and Dylan Thomas, deliberately supplement a perfect rhyme scheme with an *imperfect* or *slant rhyme* scheme. What is an imperfect or slant rhyme?

    (A) A rhyme scheme that is deliberately unfinished, or made to appear incomplete, usually for a dramatic or suspenseful effect

    (B) A rhyme scheme in which corresponding vowel sounds are only approximate, and sometimes the rhymed consonants are similar rather than identical

    (C) A rhyme scheme that represents a spontaneous overflowing of human emotions and thus seems hastily written or biased in its content

    (D) A rhyme scheme that intentionally sacrifices the lyrical rhyme scheme in order to emphasize the importance of its social or political content.

Read the following excerpt from Robert Frost's "The Figure a Poem Makes," then answer questions 42 and 43.

No tears in the writer, no tears in the reader. No surprise for the writer, no surprise for the reader. For me the initial delight is in the surprise of remembering something I didn't know I knew. I am in a place, in a situation, as if I had materialized from cloud or risen out of the ground. There is a glad recognition of the long lost and the rest follows. Step by step the wonder of unexpected supply keeps growing. The impressions most useful to my purpose seem always those I was unaware of and so made no note of at the time when taken, and the conclusion is come to that like giants we are always hurling experience ahead of us to pave the future with against the day when we may want to strike a line of purpose across it for somewhere. The line will have the more charm for not being mechanically straight. We enjoy the straight crookedness of a good walking stick. Modern instruments of precision are being used to make things crooked as if by eye and hand in the old days.

42. When Frost writes, "No tears in the writer, no tears in the reader," he is actually suggesting that

    (A) a poem that is sad or depressing in content will have a lasting or meaningful impression on readers.

    (B) a poem about human suffering or social corruption can affect or influence modern-day readers to read more poetry.

    (C) regardless of subject matter, a poem must be sincere and meaningful to the author before it will be sincere or meaningful to the reader.

    (D) he is frustrated because modern precision instruments are being used to make things appear crooked, thus seemingly replicating handmade items.

43. When Frost writes, "For me the initial delight is in the surprise of remembering something I didn't know I knew," he is actually saying

    (A) that even a poem about the most simple or humble subject matter will move or surprise the reader, if it is written with enthusiasm.

(B) the poet consciously or unconsciously writes poems based on the influential poetry he or she has read in his or her earlier years.

(C) the act of writing poetry is an enlightening and cathartic experience for the poet and thus will be enlightening to the reader.

(D) that he is getting older and it is getting more difficult for him to remember his past. Thus, poetry helps him remember things.

44. A literary symbol is

(A) a word or phrase that signifies an object or event which in turn signifies something else, or offers a range of interpretations beyond itself.

(B) a round concave brass plate that produces a loud sound when struck with a stick or other stiff object.

(C) a word or phrase that refers or represents other genres of literary styles of writing.

(D) anything that motivates a character or moves a story or poem forward, rather than simply allowing the writing to remain stagnant.

45. Alliteration is

(A) another name for a literary style or structure that uses bright colors to represent ideas or feelings.

(B) a word (or series of words) like *buzz* that resembles the sound it denotes.

(C) a word, verse, or sentence that reads the same backward or forward.

(D) the repetition of usually initial consonant sounds in two or more neighboring words or syllables.

46. Cavalier poets such as Richard Lovelace, Thomas Carew, and Robert Herrick called themselves "Sons of Ben." Who is the "Ben" they refer to?

    (A) Ben Franklin

    (B) Uncle Ben

    (C) Ben Jonson

    (D) Ben Cartwright

47. The Latin phrase *carpe diem* is a familiar paradigm generally associated with the Cavalier poets. What is the translation for *carpe diem*?

    (A) Seize the love.

    (B) Seize the woman.

    (C) Seize the youth.

    (D) Seize the day.

48. Narrative points of view are influential in the interpretation of both poetry and prose. Which of the following examples is an example of a third-person omniscient narrator?

    (A) When I walked into the room, I was overcome with a strange feeling of familiarity. Although I'd never been there before, I felt as if I had.

    (B) You know the feeling you get when you walk into a room for the first time, yet you feel as if you'd been there before.

    (C) He walked into the room for the first time, yet he was overcome with a feeling of peculiar familiarity.

    (D) I walked into the room and was overcome with a strange feeling of familiarity. I wondered if I'd been there before.

49. While ambiguous writing can be a stumbling block for many novice authors, seasoned veterans of the craft, from Shakespeare to Joyce, use ambiguity for pluralistic effects. What does *ambiguous* mean?

    (A) Using a vague or ambivalent word or expression when a precise word or phrase is called for

    (B) Using a literary text or reference, without explicit identification of the text or reference

    (C) Using a word or phrase that states specifically what the author is trying to say

    (D) Using a literary text or reference that stipulates the continuity of the jargon in a juxtaposing intertextuality

50. John Donne, John Keats, and a myriad of poets use apostrophes for dramatic or rhetorical effect. What is an apostrophe?

    (A) A mark or symbol used to indicate the omission of letters, or to indicate the possessive case, or the plural

    (B) A question that is asked not to receive information or an answer, but for the purposes of substantiating an argument

    (C) A fictional representation in a verbal medium of beings thinking, feeling, acting, and interacting

    (D) A direct and explicit address either to an absent person or to an abstract or nonhuman entity

Practice Test 1, Subtest I
Answer Key Chart & Codes

Question	Answer	SMR Code
1	C	1.1 Literary Analysis
2	D	1.2 Literary Elements
3	A	1.1 Literary Analysis
4	B	1.2 Literary Elements
5	B	1.3 Literary Criticism
6	D	1.3 Literary Criticism
7	A	1.1 Literary Analysis
8	D	1.2 Literary Elements
9	C	1.2 Literary Elements
10	B	1.1 Literary Analysis
11	A	1.2 Literary Elements
12	D	1.1 Literary Analysis
13	A	1.2 Literary Elements
14	B	1.2 Literary Elements
15	C	1.1 Literary Analysis
16	D	1.1 Literary Analysis
17	D	1.1 Literary Analysis
18	B	1.2 Literary Elements
19	C	1.3 Literary Criticism
20	A	1.3 Literary Criticism
21	C	1.1 Literary Analysis
22	D	1.3 Literary Criticism
23	B	1.3 Literary Criticism
24	D	1.1 Literary Analysis
25	C	1.3 Literary Criticism
26	D	3.2 Rhetorical Features of Literary & Non-Literary Oral and Written Tests
27	A	3.1 Written Composing Processes
28	A	3.3 Rhetorical Effects of Grammatical Elements
29	C	3.2 Rhetorical Features of Literary & Non-Literary Oral and Written Tests
30	B	3.4 Conventions of Oral & Written Language

Question	Answer	SMR Code
31	A	3.5 Research Strategies
32	B	3.3 Rhetorical Effects of Grammatical Elements
33	D	3.5 Research Strategies
34	C	3.4 Conventions of Oral & Written Language
35	A	3.2 Rhetorical Features of Literary & Non-Literary Oral and Written Tests
36	B	3.5 Research Strategies
37	D	3.1 Written Composing Processes
38	C	3.4 Conventions of Oral & Written Language
39	B	3.3 Rhetorical Effects of Grammatical Elements
40	A	3.4 Conventions of Oral & Written Language
41	B	3.4 Conventions of Oral & Written Language
42	C	3.5 Research Strategies
43	C	3.5 Research Strategies
44	A	3.3 Rhetorical Effects of Grammatical Elements
45	D	3.2 Rhetorical Features of Literary & Non-Literary Oral and Written Tests
46	C	1.2 Literary Elements
47	D	1.2 Literary Elements
48	C	3.2 Rhetorical Features of Literary & Non-Literary Oral and Written Tests
49	A	3.1 Written Composing Processes
50	D	3.1 Written Composing Processes

Practice Test 1, Subtest I Progress Chart: Multiple-Choice Questions

Subtest 1: Literary Analysis SMR Code 1.1

1C__ 3A__ 7A__ 10B__ 12D__ 15C__ 16D__ 17 D__ 21C__ 24D__   __/10

Literary Elements SMR Code 1.2

2D__ 4B__ 8D__ 9C__ 11A__ 13A__ 14B__ 18B__ 46C__ 47D__   __/10

Literary Criticism SMR Code 1.3

5B__ 6D__ 19C__ 20A__ 22D__ 23B__ 25C__   __/7

Written Composing Processes SMR Code 3.1

27A__ 37D__ 49A__ 50D__   __/4

**Rhetorical Features of Literary & Non-literary
Oral & Written Tests SMR Code 3.2**

26D__ 29C__ 35A__ 45D__ 48C__   __/5

Rhetorical Effects of Grammatical Elements SMR Code 3.3

28A__ 32B__ 39B__ 44A__   __/4

Conventions of Oral & Written Language SMR Code 3.4

30B__ 34C__ 38C__ 40A__ 41B__   __/5

Research Strategies SMR Code 3.5

31A__ 33D__ 36B__ 42C__ 43C__   __/5

Subtest I (SMR Codes 1.1 to 1.3; 3.1 to 3.5)   Total __/50

Practice Test 1, Subtest I
Detailed Explanations of Answers

1. **(C)** (SMR 1.1)
   Conventionally speaking, when authors and poets use a word repeatedly, as Coleridge does with "water," it emphasizes the abstract or symbolic aspect of the language. Thus, (C), Coleridge uses water as a symbolic representation.

2. **(D)** (SMR 1.2)
   Water is traditionally thought of as (D), an abundant life-giving element. Symbolically, "water," has come to represent food, a source and supply of, safety (Moses is saved by placing him in water), infra structure as in the transportation of goods and people, sanitation and personal hygiene, as well as recreational activities: all of which combine to suggest an abundant life-giving element.

3. **(A)** (SMR 1.1)
   Coleridge places the Mariner in a vast surrounding of water not yet fit for human consumption, because he is emphasizing the aspect that while physical, spiritual, and emotional nourishment surrounds us, people for various reasons are not always capable or willing to assess it. Thus, the correct answer is (A).

4. **(B)** (SMR 1.2)
   As being in nature is a cathartic experience to the Romantics, there needs to be a one-on-one relationship with no other distractions.

5. **(B)** (SMR 1.3)
   Romantic poets are inspired by nature, and that impulse is then crafted into a work of art. That is, the inception of the poem is based on spontaneity while the actual poem itself is a work of art.

6. **(D)** (SMR 1.3)
   Crane, like many American authors, grapples with the idea of nature versus nurture.

7. **(A)** (SMR 1.1)
   Think of realism as a literary attempt at photography—a realistic representation as opposed to a romantic one.

8. **(D)** (SMR 1.2)
Regional writing—local color—is the literary use of distinctive characteristics and/or idiosyncrasies of a particular locality and/or its inhabitants.

9. **(C)** (SMR 1.2)
An epic poem is a long narrative poem on a serious subject told in a formal and/or elevated style centering on a heroic figure.

10. **(B)** (SMR 1.1)
Kafka uses hunger as a metaphor for organized religion and spirituality. Author's note: You may recall that Kafka was born in Prague, and thus his original manuscripts, like many other literary masterpieces, are written in a language other than English (in this case, Czechoslovakian). So I've included a second version of the opening paragraph because it's important that you remember that variations in translations are also an important element in literary interpretation. When you have a moment compare the subtle (or not so subtle) variations in the two versions. The second is given below. Consider how these variations might influence your literary interpretation(s).

> In the last decades interest in hunger artists has declined considerably. Whereas in earlier days there was good money to be earned putting on major productions of this sort under one's own management, nowadays that is totally impossible. Those were different times. Back then the hunger artist captured the attention of the entire city. From day to day while the fasting lasted, participation increased. Everyone wanted to see the hunger artist at least daily. During the final days there were people with subscription tickets who sat all day in front of the small barred cage. And there were even viewing hours at night, their impact heightened by torchlight. On fine days the cage was dragged out into the open air, and then the hunger artist was put on display particularly for the children. While for grown-ups the hunger artist was often merely a joke, something they participated in because it was fashionable, the children looked on amazed, their mouths open, holding each other's hands for safety, as he sat there on scattered straw—spurning a chair—in a black tights, looking pale, with his ribs sticking out prominently, sometimes nodding politely, answering questions with a forced smile, even sticking his arm out through the bars to let people feel how emaciated he was, but then completely sinking back into himself, so that he paid no attention to anything, not even to what was so important to him, the striking of the clock, which was the single furnishing in the cage, merely looking out in front of him with his eyes almost shut and now and then sipping from a tiny glass of water to moisten his lips.

Ian Johnston, trans. Malaspina University-College, Nanaimo, British Columbia, Canada, released October 2003. Johnston's translation is in the public domain and may be used by anyone, in whole or in part, without permission and without charge, provided the source is acknowledged.

11. **(A)** (SMR 1.2)

Grown-ups view him as a joke. While the text supports this conclusion—substantiating evidence can be found in, *The Norton Introduction to Literature*, 7ᵗʰ ed. *Instructor's Guide*, New York, WW Norton, 1998—"Less obvious…is the idea that the hunger artist represents a religious figure of some sort or, in slightly different terms, the spiritual side of humankind, the soul…" (60)

12. **(D)** (SMR 1.1)

Geoffrey Chaucer used this poetic style in the *Canterbury Tales* and *The Legend of Good Women*.

13. **(A)** (SMR 1.2)

A sonnet is a lyric poem consisting of a single stanza of fourteen lines of iambic pentameter linked by an intricate rhyme scheme.

14. **(B)** (SMR 1.2)

A soliloquy is a monologue in which an actor speaks their thoughts and feelings aloud.

15. **(C)** (SMR 1.1)

Scholars credit Homer, a Greek poet, with writing *The Iliad* and *The Odyssey*.

16. **(D)** (SMR 1.1)

The art of transmitting culture, beliefs, heritage, mythologies, and so on, either in the form of prose and verse, by word of mouth is also known as oral tradition.

17. **(D)** (SMR 1.1)

John Donne is considered by many to be the archetype of the Metaphysical poets.

18. **(B)** (SMR 1.2)

The word *pathos* is derived from the Greek term, meaning "to experience suffering or emotion."

19. **(C)** (SMR 1.3)

An effective persuasive argument muse include a full recognition and clear analysis of the counterargument showing its strengths and weaknesses.

20. **(A)** (SMR 1.3)

Paraphrasing is a legitimate and effective tool in establishing a comprehensive argument.

21. **(C)** (SMR 1.1)

    An anecdote is a short narrative of an interesting, amusing, or biographical incident that serves to elucidate a point or idea.

22. **(D)** (SMR 1.3)

    Douglass's thesis can be paraphrased as "If the right [of quality] belongs to any, it belongs to all."

23. **(B)** (SMR 1.3)

    Answers (A) and (C) relate to owning a franchise such as a McDonald's. Answer (D) is akin to the definition for *frankness*.

24. **(D)** (SMR 1.1)

    The association between Mark Twain and the Mississippi River is undeniable.

25. **(C)** (SMR 1.3)

    Ambrose Bierce began his writing career as a newspaper journalist.

26. **(D)** (SMR 3.2)

    A syllogism consists of a major premise, a minor premise, and a conclusion.

27. **(A)** (SMR 3.1)

    A rhetorical argument using deductive reasoning builds from accepted truths to specific conclusions.

28. **(A)** (SMR 3.3)

    According to Aristotelian logic, the use of narrative is an effect form of argument that "should not be considered innocent moments of entertainment in political communication."

29. **(C)** (SMR 3.2)

    Logos is a rhetorical argument based on logic. In this example, the speaker is using a logical progression known as a syllogism, consisting of a major premise (not enough money for transit system), a minor premise (our city's economy is dependant on this transit system), and a logical conclusion (therefore, we need to raise money (taxes) to maintain/upgrade the system)." We do not have enough money to pay for improvements to our transit system. And without such civic improvements, this transportation system will weaken and thus hinder our economy. Therefore, we should raise taxes to pay for a better transit system.

30. **(B)** (SMR 3.4)
A metaphor is an example of figurative language.

31. **(A)** (SMR 3.5)
T. S. Eliot's *The Waste Land* is a poetic example of modernism.

32. **(B)** (SMR 3.3)
Answer (A) is the definition for *metonymy*, (C) is the definition for *kenning*, and (D) is the definition for *poetic conceit*.

33. **(D)** (SMR 3.5)
New historicism is a form of literary theory whereby critics focus primarily on the historical and cultural conditions under which the literature was produced.

34. **(C)** (SMR 3.4)
The overall tone of the poem is one of gratitude and irony. Perhaps, but the language of gratitude spoken on the part of a slave " 'TWAS mercy brought me from my Pagan land," makes the irony rather self-evident (?) doesn't it?

35. **(A)** (SMR 3.2)
The poem is written in couplets.

36. **(B)** (SMR 3.5)
Postcolonial literatures study the interactions between European nations and the societies they colonized in the modern period. These works often involve the political, social, and cultural independence of peoples formerly subjugated in colonial empires.

37. **(D)** (SMR 3.1)
Answer (A) is a satire, (B) is a parable, and (C) is a repartee.

38. **(C)** (SMR 3.4)
A topic sentence, usually located at the beginning of a paper, states the main premise of an essay.

39. **(B)** (SMR 3.3)
An epistolary novel is an extended fictional narrative, written in the form of letters, diaries, and journal entries.

40. **(A)** (SMR 3.4)
Answer (B) defines *pastoral*, (C) defines *pantomime*, and (D), *paranormal*.

41. **(B)** (SMR 3.4)
An imperfect, or slant rhyme is a rhyme scheme n which corresponding vowel sounds are only approximate, and sometimes the rhymed consonants are similar rather than identical.

42. **(C)** (SMR 3.5)
Frost is suggesting that regardless of subject matter, a poem must be sincere and meaningful to the author before it will be sincere or meaningful to the reader.

43. **(C)** (SMR 3.5)
Frost is saying that the act of writing poetry is an enlightening and cathartic experience for the poet, and thus will be enlightening for the reader.

44. **(A)** (SMR 3.3)
A literary symbol is a word or phrase that signifies an object or event which in turn signifies something else, or offers a range of interpretations beyond itself.

45. **(D)** (SMR 3.2)
Answer (A) is a component of impressionism, (B) defines *onomatopoeia*, and (C) defines *palindrome*.

46. **(C)** (SMR 1.2)
The expression "Sons of Ben" refers to Ben Jonson. "Jonson (1572 – 1637), a poet, playwright, and scholar, was the dean and the leading wit of the group of writers who gathered at the *Mermaid Tavern* in the Cheapside district of London. The young poets influenced by Jonson were the self-styled 'sons' or 'tribe' of Ben, later called the *Cavalier poets*, a group which included, among others, *Robert Herrick, Thomas Carew, Sir John Suckling*, and *Richard Lovelace*."
Source:
Jokinen, Anniina. "The Life of Ben Jonson". *Luminarium*.
9 Sept 2003. [Page accessed – 9/19/07].
<http://www.luminarium.org/sevenlit/jonson/benbio.htm>

47. **(D)** (SMR 1.2)
Carpe diem means "seize the day."

48. **(C)** (SMR 3.2)
Answer (A) is a first-person point of view, (B) is a second-person narration, and (D) is a first-person limited narration.

49. **(A)** (SMR 3.1)
Answer (B) describes *allusion*, (C) describes a concrete word or phrase, and (D) is an erroneous example of ambiguous writing.

50. **(D)** (SMR 3.1)
Answer (A) is a punctuation mark, also known as an apostrophe. It is a homonym for the correct response which in this case is, "Apostrophe" as an extended metaphor, or an address to an absent person or to an abstract or nonhuman entity. (B) is a rhetorical question, (C) is the definition for *rhetoric*.

Practice Test 1

Subtest II –
Language, Linguistics, and Literacy

This practice test is also on CD-ROM in our special interactive CSET: English TEST*ware*®. It is highly recommended that you first take this exam on computer. You will then have the additional study features and benefits of enforced timed conditions and instant, accurate scoring. See page xvii for instructions on how to get the most out of REA's TEST*ware*®.

Practice Test 1, Subtest II
Answer Sheet

1. Ⓐ Ⓑ Ⓒ Ⓓ
2. Ⓐ Ⓑ Ⓒ Ⓓ
3. Ⓐ Ⓑ Ⓒ Ⓓ
4. Ⓐ Ⓑ Ⓒ Ⓓ
5. Ⓐ Ⓑ Ⓒ Ⓓ
6. Ⓐ Ⓑ Ⓒ Ⓓ
7. Ⓐ Ⓑ Ⓒ Ⓓ
8. Ⓐ Ⓑ Ⓒ Ⓓ
9. Ⓐ Ⓑ Ⓒ Ⓓ
10. Ⓐ Ⓑ Ⓒ Ⓓ
11. Ⓐ Ⓑ Ⓒ Ⓓ
12. Ⓐ Ⓑ Ⓒ Ⓓ
13. Ⓐ Ⓑ Ⓒ Ⓓ
14. Ⓐ Ⓑ Ⓒ Ⓓ
15. Ⓐ Ⓑ Ⓒ Ⓓ
16. Ⓐ Ⓑ Ⓒ Ⓓ
17. Ⓐ Ⓑ Ⓒ Ⓓ
18. Ⓐ Ⓑ Ⓒ Ⓓ
19. Ⓐ Ⓑ Ⓒ Ⓓ
20. Ⓐ Ⓑ Ⓒ Ⓓ
21. Ⓐ Ⓑ Ⓒ Ⓓ
22. Ⓐ Ⓑ Ⓒ Ⓓ
23. Ⓐ Ⓑ Ⓒ Ⓓ
24. Ⓐ Ⓑ Ⓒ Ⓓ
25. Ⓐ Ⓑ Ⓒ Ⓓ

26. Ⓐ Ⓑ Ⓒ Ⓓ
27. Ⓐ Ⓑ Ⓒ Ⓓ
28. Ⓐ Ⓑ Ⓒ Ⓓ
29. Ⓐ Ⓑ Ⓒ Ⓓ
30. Ⓐ Ⓑ Ⓒ Ⓓ
31. Ⓐ Ⓑ Ⓒ Ⓓ
32. Ⓐ Ⓑ Ⓒ Ⓓ
33. Ⓐ Ⓑ Ⓒ Ⓓ
34. Ⓐ Ⓑ Ⓒ Ⓓ
35. Ⓐ Ⓑ Ⓒ Ⓓ
36. Ⓐ Ⓑ Ⓒ Ⓓ
37. Ⓐ Ⓑ Ⓒ Ⓓ
38. Ⓐ Ⓑ Ⓒ Ⓓ
39. Ⓐ Ⓑ Ⓒ Ⓓ
40. Ⓐ Ⓑ Ⓒ Ⓓ
41. Ⓐ Ⓑ Ⓒ Ⓓ
42. Ⓐ Ⓑ Ⓒ Ⓓ
43. Ⓐ Ⓑ Ⓒ Ⓓ
44. Ⓐ Ⓑ Ⓒ Ⓓ
45. Ⓐ Ⓑ Ⓒ Ⓓ
46. Ⓐ Ⓑ Ⓒ Ⓓ
47. Ⓐ Ⓑ Ⓒ Ⓓ
48. Ⓐ Ⓑ Ⓒ Ⓓ
49. Ⓐ Ⓑ Ⓒ Ⓓ
50. Ⓐ Ⓑ Ⓒ Ⓓ

Practice Test 1, Subtest II
Language, Linguistics, and Literacy

1. What is the definition of *grammar*?

   (A) The branch of language study or linguistic study that deals with the means of showing the relationship between words in use

   (B) The branch of language study or linguistic study that deals with the specific origins of word roots and their evolution to current and proper usage

   (C) The branch of language study or linguistic study that deals with the plant or animal world

   (D) The branch of language study or linguistic study that deals with the accuracy of dictionary entries

2. According to the branch of linguistics known as *morphology*, what is a suffix?

   (A) A punctuation point that designates the end of a sentence

   (B) A form of *affix* that follows the *morpheme* to which it attaches

   (C) A form of etymology that denotes word origins

   (D) A style of writing used by professional writers to embellish content

3. Syntax is

   (A) a division of linguistics that studies synonyms.

   (B) a monetary charge applied to recreational goods, services, and activities.

   (C) a physiological inability to form and/or comprehend coherent sentences.

   (D) the order and arrangement of words or symbols forming a logical sentence.

4. Which of the following sentences contains a double-plural noun?

   (A) We ain't got nowhere to go.

   (B) I have two rabbits.

   (C) I don't know which to choose, the green or blue one.

   (D) Where should we go, Detroit or St. Louis?

5. Irregular verbs

   (A) show a vowel alteration when changing to past tense, as in *take/took*.

   (B) show the difference between a noun and a verb, as in *swim/swimming*.

   (C) show the difficulty in linguistic studies.

   (D) belong in a zoo.

6. According to the study of phonetics, what is a fricative?

   (A) A harsh or abrasive sounding word

   (B) A word that can be used as either a noun or a verb

   (C) A consonant sound made by passing a continuous stream of air through a narrow passage in the vocal tract, creating sounds like *f* and *v*

   (D) A morpheme that alters the context of a word while maintaining the integrity of the root word

7. Alveolar sounds are those that are

   (A) articulated at the alveolar ridge, the long ridge just behind and about the upper teeth.

   (B) articulated at the alveolar ridge, the lower part of the larynx.

(C)   articulated at the alveolar ridge, produced by passing air through the nasal passages.

(D)   articulated at the alveolar ridge, the part of the diaphragm that pushes wind over the vocal cords.

8.   Semantically speaking, *homonymy* refers to

(A)   words having identical expression (sound) or pronunciation but different meanings, as in *book* a flight, read a *book*.

(B)   words in a sentence that begin with a repeating consonant sound, as in *Peter Piper picked a peck of pickled peppers.*

(C)   words that sound different but have the same meanings, as in *sea* and *ocean*.

(D)   figurative language that combines two words into one, creating an aesthetic metaphor, as in *whale road*, meaning "ocean."

9.   What is a morpheme?

(A)   A word that combines other words and establishes its own meaning, as in *businessman* (*business* + *man*)

(B)   A word that changes from a noun to a verb when *-ing* is added, as in *swim/swimming*

(C)   A quantitative noun that changes spelling when going from singular to plural, as in *mouse/mice*

(D)   The smallest unit of language that has meaning or serves a grammatical function, for example *cat*.

10. An affix, also known as a *bound morpheme*,

    (A) attaches to a word, thus giving it the opposite connotation from its original meaning; for example, *non-* added to *negotiable* creates the word *nonnegotiable.*

    (B) attaches to a root or stem morpheme, and can be either prefix or a suffix.

    (C) attaches to a verb, thereby making it an adverb; for example, *-ly* added to *swift* creates the adverb *swiftly.*

    (D) attaches words via a hyphen, as in *twenty-first-century.*

11. A *diphthong* is

    (A) a fluctuation in the pronunciation of consonant sounds, produced by regulating airflow over the vocal cords.

    (B) a vowel sound whose production requires the tongue to start in one place and move (or glide) to another.

    (C) a consonant sound produced by the fluttering of the tongue behind the upper teeth.

    (D) an extended vowel sound whose production is created by slowly releasing air over the vocal cords.

12. Prior to the development of written languages, stories, culture, and traditions were passed down from one generation to the next via

    (A) pictures painted on walls, rocks, and other surfaces, also known as *pictography.*

    (B) carvings, drawings, and sand designs, also known as *cartography.*

    (C) word of mouth, also known as *oral tradition.*

    (D) a series of elaborate gestures, hand signs, and facial expressions, also known as *etymology.*

13. What is a metaphor?

    (A) A figure of speech containing an implied comparison in which a word or phrase ordinarily and primarily used for one thing is applied to another, as in *All the world's a stage*.

    (B) A figure of speech containing contemporary representation of linguistic ideology, primarily used by fiction writers, as in *That car is phat*.

    (C) A figure of speech containing a reproduction of the sounds that the word is supposed to represent, as in *buzz*.

    (D) A figure of speech containing the implied thematic representation of a story, fable, or morality tale, as in *Slow and steady wins the race*.

14. When two different words share the same or similar meaning, they are

    (A) obsequies.
    (B) onomatopoeias.
    (C) homophones.
    (D) synonyms.

15. The verb and its related words in a clause or sentence is more commonly referred to as a

    (A) verb clause.
    (B) noun clause.
    (C) predicate.
    (D) postulate.

16. Before the invention of oral tradition and writing, people

    (A) painted visual symbols on rock formations to tell stories and record events.

    (B) carved small tokens or "fetishes" to represent important people and places, and to record events.

    (C) used hieroglyphs to tell stories and record events.

    (D) communicated via elaborate pantomime gestures and movements.

17. The phonetic alphabet

    (A) represents sound in a visual fashion, assigning a simple iconic picture to each sound allowing it to be represented visually.

    (B) represents sound in a way whereby each sound, regardless of language, is assigned a distinct representation, independent of standard or traditional alphabet.

    (C) represents a lack of effort on the part of orthographies to dissect each linguistic sound phonetically, rather than visually.

    (D) represents an antiquated culture whose linguistic properties have long since been lost to time.

18. All languages contain two basic sound types. What are they?

    (A) Affricates and fricatives

    (B) Flotsam and jetsam

    (C) Phrases and clauses

    (D) Consonants and vowels

19. A hybrid language used for communication between different cultures that interact but otherwise do not share a common language, is known as

    (A) indigenous language.

    (B) pidgin English.

    (C) Pig Latin.

    (D) lingua franca.

20. According to the principle of language acquisition, the first aspects of maturation required for a child's language acquisition are the ability to

    (A) form and hold mental pictures, that is, the ability to form, recognize, and use symbols.

    (B) form and generate basic vowel and consonant sounds, such as *dada* and *mama*.

    (C) grasp abstract concepts and special relations, for example, pointing at a glass of water when thirsty.

    (D) generalize abstract concepts such as water in a cup, in the bathtub, and from a faucet.

21. According to the National Institute for Literacy, parents and educators "can encourage indirect vocabulary learning by first

    (A) reading aloud to your children, regardless of age or grade level."

    (B) showing pictures to your children and mimicking the sounds associated with those pictures."

    (C) allowing children to watch television shows designed to promote juvenile learning."

    (D) exposing infants and very young children to classical music."

22. According to the National Institute for Literacy, "A program of systematic phonics instruction

    (A) clearly identifies a carefully selected and useful set of letter–sound relationships and then organizes the introduction of those relationships into logical instructional sequences."

    (B) clearly articulates a random series of ideas, needs, and principles based primarily on the basic needs of infants and toddlers."

    (C) clearly acknowledges that children independently learn language at various levels and stages of development, thus relieving the pressure from parents and educators to 'push' the child into premature conversations."

    (D) clearly expresses the need for infants and toddlers to express their immediate wants and needs in a verbal fashion, establishing a basic cause and effect relationship in the child's mind."

23. Which of the following sentences contains an example of a gerund?

    (A) Mother wouldn't say whether we could go to the game on Saturday night.

    (B) Mother walks us to school every day.

    (C) Mother objected to our swimming only 30 minutes after eating.

    (D) Mother thinks I am the star of the team, even though I was picked last.

24. Select the sentence below that shows a relative clause embedded as a restrictive clause.

    (A) These paintings are beautiful.
    (B) Every color has a different hue.
    (C) I will put them in frames for display on my walls.
    (D) Thank you for this wonderful artwork.

25. Prepositional phrases often serve as adverbs. Which of the following sentences includes a prepositional phrase serving as an adverb?

    (A) The police followed the robber until they had enough evidence to convict him.

    (B) The police followed the robber because they knew he was guilty.

    (C) The police followed the robber through the deserted city streets.

    (D) The police followed the robber while his trail was still hot.

26. A colon tells the reader that what follows is closely related to the preceding clause. Which of the following sentences uses the colon correctly?

    (A) A dedicated artist: requires brushes, paint, canvas, and an eye for beauty.

    (B) A dedicated artist requires four things: brushes, paint, canvas, and an eye for beauty.

    (C) A dedicated artist requires materials such as paint: brushes; canvas, and an eye for beauty.

    (D) A dedicated artist requires materials consisting of paint, brushes, canvas: and an eye for beauty.

27. When a verbal phrase does not refer to a specific noun or noun phrase, it's known as a

    (A) dangling modifier.
    (B) past participle.
    (C) predicate.
    (D) independent clause.

28. The following sentence has a dangling modifier: *Last night I shot an elephant in my pajamas.* Which of the following best corrects the sentence?

    (A) I shot an elephant last night.

    (B) An elephant was wearing my pajamas when I shot him.

    (C) Last night, while I was wearing my pajamas, I shot an elephant.

    (D) Elephants don't wear pajamas.

29. To avoid ambiguity in sentences one must position words to show their relationships. Read the following sentence, then choose the answer that best rephrases the sentence to maintain continuity of thought.

    He noticed a large stain in the rug that was right in the center.

    (A) He noticed a large rug in the center of the room.

    (B) He noticed a large stain right in the center of the rug that was in the middle of the room.

    (C) He noticed a large stain right in the center of the rug.

    (D) He noticed a rug that had a large stain on it.

30. Simple and perfect verb tenses also have progressive forms. Which of the following sentences is an example of a present progressive verb form?

    (A) David is writing a novel.
    (B) David wrote a novel last year.
    (C) David will be writing a novel next year.
    (D) David is thinking about writing a novel.

31. Philology, a lexiconical descendant of *logos*, is related to literary interpretation in what way?

    (A) The study of literary texts in a logical, scholarly, and orderly fashion

(B) The study of literary texts for the purposes of authentication and interpretation

(C) The study of literary texts with a focus on iconic images and representation

(D) The study of literary texts based on the teachings and principles of Platonic logic and reasoning

32. What is the definition of *literacy*?

(A) A good thing for children to establish early in life

(B) Essential to functioning well in a wide variety of situations

(C) The ability to write prose and poetry in a manner that listeners and readers find pleasing

(D) The ability to comprehend what one reads and writes

33. An important technique for proper literary assessment is to

(A) have students read and reread various texts until they comprehend the symbolic representations.

(B) have students articulate what they have read.

(C) watch and document students, noting the ones who are eager to read.

(D) watch students' performances in authentic learning situations.

34. Subordinators introduce embedded clauses. In the sentence, *We were shocked that Bob hit the home run*, the subordinator is

(A) were
(B) that
(C) shocked
(D) hit

35. A hyponym is a word whose referent is totally included in the referent of another word. So a hyponym of *color* would be

    (A) red

    (B) hue

    (C) chroma

    (D) intensity

36. Usually it is more effective to write active rather than passive sentences. A passive sentence puts

    (A) the noun before its article.

    (B) the object before the subject.

    (C) the subject before the object.

    (D) the noun before the verb.

37. If a sentence's subject is contained in a noun phrase, then a sentence's predicate must contain which of the following?

    (A) Additional information pertaining to the noun

    (B) An antecedent

    (C) A verb phrase

    (D) An article

38. When a word is produced by a puff of air, such as the *p* sound in *pot*, the sound is said to be

    (A) aspirated.

    (B) aesthetic.

    (C) antithetical.

    (D) artificial.

39. Cognates are

   (A) not to be used in conjunction with certain pronouns.

   (B) words or morphemes that contain ambiguous lexical meanings.

   (C) appropriate when used in academic writing, but not appropriate for lyrical writing.

   (D) words or morphemes that have developed from a single etymological source or root word.

40. To express coordinate ideas in similar form, some words require a particular preposition in certain idiomatic uses. Thus,

   (A) when such words are joined in a compound construction, all the appropriate prepositions must be included, unless they are the same.

   (B) when such words are joined in a compound construction, all the appropriate noun phrases must be followed by a predicate, which contains a preposition.

   (C) when such words are joined in a compound construction, all the appropriate prepositions must support the initial article.

   (D) when such words are joined in a compound construction, all the appropriate prepositions must pertain to the thematic representation of the principal noun phrase.

41. The rule for applying a preposition or an article to all members of a series is

   (A) that you must either use the preposition or article only before the first term or else repeat it before every term.

   (B) that you must use the preposition or article any time a noun or verb phrase is used, regardless of its location in the sentence.

   (C) variable, depending on the members of a series and their relationship to the preposition or article.

   (D) that both articles and prepositions never appear together in a sentence containing a series.

42. In order for words in a sentence to show their relationship to one another, thus avoiding ambiguity, you must

    (A) bring together words and groups of words that are related in thought and keep apart those words that are not related.

    (B) bring together the words or groups of words in the noun phrase to the predicate.

    (C) bring the antecedent to its corresponding modifier, regardless of its location in the sentence.

    (D) bring the morpheme to the modifier, rather than the modifier to the morpheme.

43. To avoid confusion, modifiers should be placed next to the words they modify. If several expressions modify the same word,

    (A) they should be placed adjacent to the verb phrase, so that the relative action of the verb is articulated.

    (B) they should be arranged so that no wrong relationship is suggested.

    (C) they should be arranged according to the cognates they modify.

    (D) they should be placed at the start of the sentence, to avoid ambiguity.

44. When paraphrasing the plot of a literary work, it is standard practice to

    (A) avoid any reference to tenses in your summarization.
    (B) summarize the piece in as few words as possible.
    (C) summarize the piece in chronological order.
    (D) summarize the piece in the present tense.

45. When writing a summary of a literary work, it is necessary to

    (A) involve yourself and the reader in the piece.
    (B) be enthusiastic about what you've read.

(C)   be objective and use a neutral tone.

(D)   sound as though you know what you're talking about.

46. In a composition on literary analysis, where is the most appropriate spot to place the author's name, the title of the piece, and the thesis or central theme of your paper?

(A)   In the last sentence of the first paragraph

(B)   In the first sentence of the first paragraph

(C)   In the last sentence of the conclusion

(D)   In the first sentence of the conclusion

47. One way of the most effective ways for readers to "engage" with the text is to

(A)   use a brightly colored highlighter to mark the significant passages.

(B)   read all the author's works and the corresponding criticisms.

(C)   annotate the text with a pencil or pen and not a highlighter.

(D)   read the entire text and then reflect on its thematic representation(s).

48. An analysis or interpretation of a literary work involves

(A)   avoiding oversimplified plot and thematic summaries.

(B)   using oversimplified plot and thematic summaries.

(C)   facts and supporting materials taken from reliable secondary sources.

(D)   a brief, general outline of the author's literary credentials.

49. When integrating quotations into your analysis, it is important to

    (A) shift the perspective from the original author's voice to your own voice.

    (B) explain your reasons for using those specific quotations.

    (C) think critically and consider the audience.

    (D) avoid shifts in verb tenses.

50. Essentially, sentences can be broken into two parts, noun phrases and verb phrases, also known as, respectively,

    (A) vowels and consonants.

    (B) aspirates and fricatives.

    (C) subjects and predicates.

    (D) flotsam and jetsam.

Practice Test 1, Subtest II
Answer Key Chart & Codes

Question	Answer	SMR Code
1	A	2.1 Human Language Structures
2	B	2.2 Acquisition & Development of Language & Literacy
3	D	2.4 Grammatical Structures of English
4	B	2.4 Grammatical Structures of English
5	A	2.4 Grammatical Structures of English
6	C	2.3 Literacy Studies
7	A	2.2 Acquisition & Development of Language & Literacy
8	A	2.3 Literacy Studies
9	D	2.1 Human Language Structures
10	B	2.1 Human Language Structures
11	B	2.4 Grammatical Structures of English
12	C	2.1 Human Language Structures
13	A	2.2 Acquisition & Development of Language & Literacy
14	D	2.4 Grammatical Structures of English
15	C	2.1 Human Language Structures
16	A	2.3 Literacy Studies
17	B	2.2 Acquisition & Development of Language & Literacy
18	D	2.1 Human Language Structures
19	D	2.1 Human Language Structures
20	A	2.3 Literacy Studies
21	A	2.2 Acquisition & Development of Language & Literacy
22	A	2.3 Literacy Studies
23	C	2.4 Grammatical Structures of English
24	C	2.4 Grammatical Structures of English
25	C	2.4 Grammatical Structures of English

Question	Answer	SMR Code
26	B	2.4 Grammatical Structures of English
27	A	2.4 Grammatical Structures of English
28	C	2.1 Human Language Structures
29	C	2.1 Human Language Structures
30	A	2.1 Human Language Structures
31	B	2.3 Literacy Studies
32	D	2.3 Literacy Studies
33	D	2.2 Acquisition & Development of Language & Literacy
34	B	2.4 Grammatical Structures of English
35	A	2.4 Grammatical Structures of English
36	B	2.4 Grammatical Structures of English
37	C	2.1 Human Language Structures
38	A	2.1 Human Language Structures
39	D	2.1 Human Language Structures
40	A	2.4 Grammatical Structures of English
41	A	2.4 Grammatical Structures of English
42	A	2.1 Human Language Structures
43	B	2.4 Grammatical Structures of English
44	D	2.2 Acquisition & Development of Language & Literacy
45	C	2.3 Literacy Studies
46	B	2.3 Literacy Studies
47	C	2.3 Literacy Studies
48	A	2.2 Acquisition & Development of Language & Literacy
49	D	2.4 Grammatical Structures of English
50	C	2.1 Human Language Structures

Practice Test 1, Subtest II Progress Chart: Multiple-Choice Questions

Human Language Structures SMR Code 2.1

1A__ 9D__ 10B__ 12C__ 15C__ 18D__ 19D__ 28C__
29C__ 30A__ 37C__ 38A__ 39D__ 42A__ 50C__   __/15

**Acquisition & Development of Language & Literacy
SMR Code 2.2**

2B__ 7A__ 13A__ 17B__ 21A__ 33D__ 44D__ 48A__   __/8

Literacy Studies SMR Code 2.3

6C__ 8A__ 16A__ 20A__ 22A__ 31B__ 32D__ 45C__ 46B__ 47C__   __/10

Grammatical Structures of English SMR Code 2.4

3D__ 4B__ 5A__ 11B__ 14D__ 23C__ 24C__ 25C__ 26B__
27A__ 34B__ 35A__ 36B__ 40A__ 41A__ 43B__ 49D__   __/17

Subtest II (SMR Codes 2.1 to 2.4)   **Total __/50**

Practice Test 1, Subtest II
Detailed Explanations of Answers

1. **(A)** (SMR 2.1)
    According to the Oxford English Dictionary, *grammar* is defined as "the branch of language study or linguistic study which deals with the means of showing the relationship between words in use."

2. **(B)** (SMR 2.2)
    Morphology refers to alterations made to a root word that give it the appropriate grammatical tense, quantity, and so forth. As suffixes such as *-ing* and *-ed* go at the end of the word, the correct answer is B.

3. **(D)** (SMR 2.4)

4. **(B)** (SMR 2.4)
    There must be an agreement between the quantity and the noun.

5. **(A)** (SMR 2.4)

6. **(C)** (SMR 2.3)
    In linguistic studies a fricative is a consonant sound made by passing a continuous stream of air through a narrow passage in the vocal tract, as opposed to, say, an affricate, which is formed in a different section of the mouth and throat, such as the *ch* sound in *choose*.

7. **(A)** (SMR 2.2)
    Also a linguistic formation of sounds, created by touching the tongue to the ridge of the teeth.

8. **(A)** (SMR 2.3)
    Homonymy is the semantic term for a word having identical expression but different meanings, such as "*book* a flight" and "read a *book*." Remember that homophones are words that sound alike but have different meanings, such as *see* and *sea*.

9. **(D)** (SMR 2.1)

Morphemes are the smallest unit that a word can be broken into. *Pin*, for example, cannot be broken into a smaller form and still have meaning.

10. **(B)** (SMR 2.1)

Affixes are also known as bound morphemes. They attach to a root or stem morpheme. A prefix, such as *-un*, attaches to the beginning of word, while a suffix, such as *-ing*, attaches to the end of a word.

11. **(B)** (SMR 2.4)

According to linguistics principles, a diphthong is a vowel sound whose production requires the tongue to start in one place and move, or glide, to another.

12. **(C)** (SMR 2.1)

Before the advent of writing as we know it, stories, culture, heritage, legends, and traditions were passed along by word of mouth, also known as oral tradition.

13. **(A)** (SMR 2.2)

A metaphor is a figure of speech containing an implied comparison in which a word or phrase ordinarily and primarily used for one thing is applied to another, for thematic, dramatic, or other type of effect, as in *All the world's a stage, and we are merely players*.

14. **(D)** (SMR 2.4)

Various words that share the same or similar meaning, for example *city* and *metropolis*, are known as synonyms.

15. **(C)** (SMR 2.1)

The predicate expresseses what the subject does, experiences, or is, for example fish *swim*, the party goers *celebrated wildly for a long time*, the graduating class *celebrated*.

16. **(A)** (SMR 2.3)

Before the invention of a writing alphabet as we know it, people communicated by painting visual symbols on rock formations to tell stories and record events.

17. **(B)** (SMR 2.2)

The phonetic alphabet represents sounds as opposed to words. Thus it is adaptable to writing all languages, because it shows the sound it represents.

18. **(D)** (SMR 2.1)

All languages contain vowel and consonant sound types. Consonants are formed by obstructing the flow of air as it passes from the lungs, while vowel sounds are formed by allowing the flow of air to pass freely from the lungs.

19. **(D)** (SMR 2.1)

A lingua franca is a system of communication providing mutual understanding among multilingual cultures. Trade centers and other venues where different cultures interact but otherwise do not share a common language require a lingua franca.

20. **(A)** (SMR 2.3)

According to the National Institute for Literacy's principles of language acquisition, children must be able to form and hold mental pictures if they are to acquire language fundamentals. Before children can develop language skills, they must first possess the ability to form and recognize symbols, along with the ability to use tools to express those symbols.

21. **(A)** (SMR 2.2)

Reading aloud to your students, regardless of age or grade level, increases vocabulary. Reading aloud also augments comprehension when you discuss the selection with your students before, during, and after they read it.

22. **(A)** (SMR 2.3)

The National Institute for Literacy states that, "A program of systematic phonics instruction clearly identifies a carefully selected and useful set of letter–sound relationships and then organizes the introduction of those relationships into a logical instructional sequence."

23. **(C)** (SMR 2.4)

Gerunds, like infinitives, are usually stated in the possessive case, such as, "Mother objected to our *swimming* only 30 minutes after eating."

24. **(C)** (SMR 2.4)

The relative clause and the noun phrase in which it is embedded form a new noun constituent, and the relative clause functions as an adjective within the new noun phrase constituent.

25. **(C)** (SMR 2.4)

Answer (C) contains the prepositional phrase *through the deserted city streets*, which serves as an adverb detailing where the police followed the robber.

26. **(B)** (SMR 2.4)
One of the most misunderstood and misused punctuation marks, the colon tells the reader that what follows is closely related to the preceding clause, as in *A dedicated artist requires four things: brushes, paint, canvas, and an eye for beauty.*

27. **(A)** (SMR 2.4)
When a verbal phrase does not refer to a specific noun or noun phrase, it's known as a *dangling modifier*.

28. **(C)** (SMR 2.1)
In the sentence *Last night I shot an elephant in my pajamas*, the prepositional phrase *in my pajamas* is meant to modify the subject *I*, not the object *elephant*. Including the information in a new clause—*while I was wearing my pajamas*—makes the sentence's meaning clear.

29. **(C)** (SMR 2.1)
In the sentence *He noticed a large stain in the rug that was right in the center*, the restrictive clause *that was right in the center* is meant to modify *stain*, not *rug*. Answer (C) correctly moves the descriptive phrase closer to the word it modifies.

30. **(A)** (SMR 2.1)
While simple and perfect verb tenses have a progressive form, verbs expressing a state of mind or mental activity generally are *not* used in the progressive form.

31. **(B)** (SMR 2.3)
Originally, *philology* referred to the love of learning, study, and scholarship, especially as it relates to the study of literary texts. Now, *Merriam-Webster's New World Dictionary* (second edition) defines *philology* as "the study of literature and of disciplines relevant to literature or to language as used in literature, especially historical and comparative linguistics [including] the study of human speech especially as the vehicle of literature and as a field of study that sheds light on cultural history."

32. **(D)** (SMR 2.3)
Literacy is not simply the ability to read and write, but the ability to comprehend and/or process what one reads and writes.

33. **(D)** (SMR 2.2)
Because various learning skills are based on environment (e.g., a student can calculate math problems in a classroom environment under controlled conditions, but

is unable to calculate the problem outside of the classroom), to successfully assess literary skills one must watch students perform in authentic, rather than controlled, environments.

34. **(B)** (SMR 2.4)
Subordinators introduce embedded clauses in order to reduce ambiguity and increase continuity. So in the sentence *We were shocked that Bob hit the homerun*, the subordinator is *that*.

35. **(A)** (SMR 2.4)
The prefix *hypo-* means "below." A *hyponym* is a word whose referent is totally included in the referent of another term. So *red* is a hyponym of *color*, just as *dog* or *cat* are hyponyms of *mammal*.

36. **(B)** (SMR 2.4)
Back to the basics on this one: Active sentences put the subject of a sentence before the object, and passive sentences put the object of a sentence before the subject.

37. **(C)** (SMR 2.1)
For a sentence to be complete, it must contain a noun or noun phrase, which serves as the sentence subject, and a verb or verb phrase, also known as the sentence's predicate. So, if a sentence's subject contains a noun phrase, then the sentence's predicate must contain a verb phrase.

38. **(A)** (SMR 2.1)
The term *aspirate* refers to breath and the inhalation and exhalation of air into and out of the lungs. When a word is produced by a puff of air, such as the *p* sound in *pot*, or the *h* sound in *house* or *hat*, the sound is said to be aspirated.

39. **(D)** (SMR 2.1)
Cognates are words that have developed from a single etymological source or root word, such as the English word *father*, the German *vater*, and the Spanish *padre*, all of which have developed out of the Indo-European *pəter*.

40. **(A)** (SMR 2.4)
To express coordinate ideas in similar form, some words require a particular preposition in certain idiomatic uses. Thus, when such words are joined in a compound construction, all the appropriate prepositions must be included, unless they are all the same.

41. **(A)** (SMR 2.4)

The rule for applying a preposition or an article to all members of a series or list is that you must either use the preposition or article only before the first term, as in *the French, Italians, Spanish, and British*, or else the preposition or article must be repeated before every entry, as in *the French, the Italians, the Spanish, and the British*.

42. **(A)** (SMR 2.1)

To avoid ambiguity in sentences, words must appear in an order that shows their relationship to one another. This is done by bringing together words and groups of words that are related in thought, while keeping apart those words and phrases that are not related. So, to correct the ambiguous sentence *You can call your mother in London and tell her about George's taking you out to dinner for only two-dollars*, rearrange the phrases to read, *For only two-dollars, you can call your mother in London and tell her about George's taking you out to dinner*.

43. **(B)** (SMR 2.4)

Again, to avoid ambiguity, modifiers should be placed next to the words they modify. If several expressions modify the same word, they should be arranged so that no wrong relationship is implied. For example, *The director said he hoped all members would give generously to the fund at the meeting of the committee yesterday* can be rearranged to read, *At the meeting of the committee yesterday, the director said he hoped all the members would give generously to the fund*.

44. **(D)** (SMR 2.2)

When paraphrasing the plot of a literary work, it is standard practice to summarize the piece in the *present tense*—for example, "Friar Tuck *joins* Robin Hood's band" —rather than refer to the story and events in the past tense.

45. **(C)** (SMR 2.3)

When writing a summary of a literary work it is necessary to remain objective and use a neutral tone.

46. **(B)** (SMR 2.3)

When writing a composition or response to a literary work, the most appropriate place to acknowledge the author's name, the title of the piece, and the central theme is in the first sentence of the essay.

47. **(C)** (SMR 2.3)

    One of the best ways for readers to engage with a text is to annotate the text with a pencil or pen, and not with a highlighter. At first this may seem contrary to popular practices, but highlighters simply mark words, while writing with a pen or pencil promotes active reading and thinking about the materials.

48. **(A)** (SMR 2.2)

    An analysis or interpretation of a literary work involves avoiding simple plot summaries, because the goal of interpretation is to accurately articulate the author's main idea and key points as briefly yet succinctly as possible.

49. **(D)** (SMR 2.4)

    When integrating quotations into your analysis, it is important to avoid shifts in verb tenses. For example, "When Sally sees Leo's casual attire, she *blushed* like a schoolgirl at her first prom," suggests that Sally "blushed" after the fact. Notice Sally's immediate response in the corrected sentence, "When Sally sees Leo's casual attire, she *blushes* like a schoolgirl at her first prom."

50. **(C)** (SMR 2.1)

    A sentences can be broken into two parts, the noun phrase, also called the subject, and the verb phrases, also called the predicate.

Practice Test 1

Subtest III – Composition and Rhetoric; Literature and Textual Analysis

This practice test is also on CD-ROM in our special interactive CSET: English TEST*ware*®. It is highly recommended that you first take this exam on computer. You will then have the additional study features and benefits of enforced timed conditions and instant, accurate scoring. See page xvii for instructions on how to get the most out of REA's TEST*ware*®.

Practice Test 1, Subtest III
Composition and Rhetoric

Practice Question 1

Write a critical essay in which you respond to the following poem. The essay must include:

- identification of theme
    — analysis noting literary techniques, including: genre features, literary elements, and rhetorical devices used to express theme
- a conclusion

LONDON

I wandered through each chartered street,
   Near where the chartered Thames does flow,
A mark in every face I meet,
   Marks of weakness, marks of woe.

In every cry of every man,
   In every infant's cry of fear,
In every voice, in every ban,
   The mind-forged manacles I hear:

How the chimney-sweeper's cry
   Every blackening church appalls,
And the hapless soldier's sigh
   Runs in blood down palace-walls.

But most, through midnight streets I hear
   How the youthful harlot's curse
Blasts the new-born infant's tear,
   And blights with plagues the marriage-hearse.

~ William Blake (1757–1827),
Songs of Innocence and Experience

Practice Question 2

Write a critical essay showing the "association, relationship, convention, or accidental resemblance" between the symbol(s) highlighted in bold lettering, and what you think it/ they represent. Illustrate your argument by referring to specific passages from the poem, where applicable. Assume that you are writing for an educated audience.

Remember, a **symbol** is "something that stands for or suggests something else by reason of relationship, association, convention, or accidental resemblance; *especially*: a visible sign of something invisible (i.e. the lion is a *symbol* of courage, the oak is a *symbol* of strength, and the railroad is a *symbol* of modernity)"

A COAT

I MADE my **song** a **coat**
Covered with embroideries
Out of old mythologies
From heel to throat;
But the fools caught it,   *5*
Wore it in the world's eyes
As though they'd wrought it.
Song, let them take it
For there's more enterprise
In walking naked.   *10*

W.B. Yeats (1865–1939).
Responsibilities and Other Poems. 1916.
http://www.bartleby.com/147/31.html

English Subtest III: Written Response Sample

When you take the CSET: English Test, Subtest III, you will be given a four-page answer packet to use for each of the questions. You will have to confine your answer to the lined space provided. You will not write your name on the paper.

Practice writing one of your answers on the following pages.

_____

_____

_____

_____

_____

_____

_____

_____

_____

_____

_____

_____

Written Response Sample Sheets *(cont'd)*

Written Response Sample Sheets *(cont'd)*

Written Response Sample Sheets *(cont'd)*

SAMPLE ESSAYS FOR PRACTICE TEST 1: SUBTEST III

Sample Response for Practice Question 1

Four-Point Response

The narrator wandering through William Blake's, "London," provides an editorialized commentary of the squalor and abysmal living conditions commonly associated with 19th-century Britain's Industrial Revolution. The narrator "wander['s]" the streets of London, implying that anywhere and everywhere he goes he is met by sad faces "marked" or filled with suffering and "woe." Essentially then, no area or social class is safe from the consequences of London's urban industrialization. Thus, from lowly "harlots" and "chimney sweeps" to "hapless soldiers," and corrupt "blackened" clergy, no social-class seems to be safe from London's environmental cruelties and economic miseries.

For the narrator, this is not just an opportunity for social exposition, but an opportunity for social commentary on what he sees as the actual cause of the Londoner's suffering: i.e. the metaphoric use of self-imposed, "mind-forg'd manacles."

To forge or fashion mental restraints, in this case, shackles or "manacles," suggests that both ignorance, as in, lack of education and lethargy, combine with one's own limited or myopic thinking, are the actual origins of the people's misery. But of course, their limited thinking prevents them from seeing their own potential for instigating change.

Without the need or obligation to solve London's social problems, the narrator is free to editorialize or commentate on the current social-conditions, while putting the responsibility for solutions squarely on the backs of those who must instigate the change and that is the Londoner's themselves. Yet death's perpetual presence permeates the poem, from birth to marriage "hearse['s], which also suggests a genuine understanding on the narrator's part that social changes are easier spoken about than brought about.

Three-Point Response

When William Blake speaks of London as a place where he is constantly finding misery and sadness in every face he meets, he is really showing a poetic version of a modern-day Sodom and Gomorrah, complete with all the grief, "misery," suffering, and perversions of its biblical namesake. Infants are crying and harlots are cursed, or perhaps are cursing, while the blackened church stands idly by and exploits the people it's there to protect, leaving the reader to speculate that Blake's London must have been a sad, lonely, corrupt, and dirty place where even the church walls are blackened and stained with unsanctified blood.

Blake seems to be suggesting that the inhabitants of London are manacled or chained to their fears and blights, thus, they are locked to their ultimate consequences and fate. This implies that while other, more righteous avenues are available to them, the inhabitants are physically and mentally prevented from following those new avenues of escape.

Blake endlessly wanders about the city, seemingly like a modern day Lot, looking for one honest "soul" and finding none, amidst a contemporary version of Sodom and Gomorrah. Also, like its biblical namesake, London seems destined for damnation and destruction, as the marriage-hearse prepares to depart across the river Jordon, thus reiterating the inevitable fate of those who are cursed to live there.

Two-Point Response

Blake goes around London only looking for the bad things he can find, and then writes a depressing poem about how sad and miserable everyone is cuz that's all he sees. He could've just taken a walk around the park or seen Big Ben or said something about how nice the weather was, or anything like pretty flowers, just so he isn't always going around feeling so sad and bad all the time. I don't think London could be all that bad cuz I've seen pictures of it and it looks really pretty. I think hes just whining and obviously wanting to feel bad rather than trying to make himself feel good about the place where he lives in.

Why would he look at all the dirty places there are in the world and than have put little babys there where no one would really put a little baby in someplace so dirty. As of course Babys are supposed to be clean and smell like baby powder.

So, I think he just wants to be depressing about how much he dosent like babys and getting married because who wants to drive a hearst at there wedding unless they are Goths or something, no one wants that. But a limo instead. Maybe Blake just had a bad marriage or got divorced recently and is down on getting married and having babys so he writes about how sad everyone is when they get married and have babys than they drive away in a hearst. Like it could be like life when youre born and live and die. I think he's just not a happy person.

One-Point Response

I don't get this poem at all. When I went to England with my mom and dad when I was a little kid- it was really fun and nice. The people were pretty friendly but it was kinda hard to understand them sometimes cuz they all have English accents. Duh!!!!! We went to buckinghoard pal-ace and saw the queens knights or something but I wanted to go on the big farist wheel that they have there by the river Times and then my mom tried to get them to laugh, but you cant and they wont laugh no matter what you do, so maybe the poem is about the kings nights who just don't laugh no matter what you do or say and they always look serious and kinda mean.

But 4 me the city of England was kinda funny because—omg—they call soccer football like they do here but its really not like football its like soccer but they call rugby! and money is called pounds like youd weigh something in the local supermarket. Its really hard 2 figure out how much something costs so my dad had a little calculator thing that told him how much itd cost in American money and elevators are called lifts. Do you know what they call a baby stroller? Prams or trams or something stupid like that…. Lol.

I don't think this poem is very good or tells a lot about England like it really is cuz its really pretty fun to go there and if blake really didnt like it very much or isn't happy there he should just move or go somewhere else on his vacation.

Sample Response for Practice Question 2

4-Point Response

A perennial top-ten hit, recorded by dozens of artists from Barbara Streisand to Bobby Sherman is a song titled, "Make your own Kind of Music." It is about personal independence, marching to your own drummer, freedom of choice, and so on. The idea of a song as a reflection of the individual and or that individual's uniqueness or creativity, is a long established symbolic representation. In the poem, A Coat, W. B. Yeats is using this familiar symbol to represent the narrator's creative individuality. After all, the narrator did create the coat himself. The fact that the narrator felt the need to make his song "a coat," suggests that for whatever reasons, he needed to both hide and protect his artistic individuality from the rest of the world, in this case, "the fools," as a coat serves both functions equally well. Yet there is an epiphany in the poem, as the narrator comes to realize that the coat, made from archaic remnants of the past ("old mythologies"), is needless if the narrator is willing to expose or express his artistic nature to the world, without concern for their critical judgments or misappropriations, That is, the Narrator is without concern for "fools" who caught and pretend they "wrought" his artistic ideas/ ideals. In conclusion, the narrator becomes aware that there is more artistic "enterprise" when he's willing to "walk naked."

3-Point Response

Yeats is telling us that his song is what makes him happy. We sing when we are happy and so his "song" is a symbol of his mental state of mind. The song works to show the reader that Yeats has a song to sing, and this shows his emotional state of mind. If Yeats puts "a coat" on his song, than he might be muffling the sound, or covering it up, to protect it and keep it out of the world's or "fools" elements. A coat is warm in the winter and keeps elements like rain and wind off of your body, so for Yeats, it's a way for him to love and protect his song. In essence, he's keeping it safe and warm. This might be showing that Yeats loves himself and his happy feelings and is willing to protect them. So if the song is a representation of himself, and the coat is a way to keep himself safe, than the poem can be showing us a form of self-love, in other words, a way to take care of yourself. Once he's comfortable in his skin, Yeats Is likely to feel more comfortable when he's showing off by walking around naked and not being ashamed.

2-Point Response

He's probably talking about a song that he's herd before on the radio like when hes driving and he feels cold and sad when he realizes that he can't remember what all the words, like "mythologies" means. What song is it he wonders? How do the words go? He isn't sure. So he puts on his "old" coat on that he made for himself a long time ago out of something called embroideries and wears it around hoping that it'll makes him feel better about himself because than he maybe can remember the words to the song he likes. It must be a long coat because he says that it covers him from his neck to his toes, so he'll be warm and happy and won't feel cold and sad anymore. Maybe it's a long song too? He dosent like foolish people he says so he'll probably wear it around inside wear no one can see him in it. Than he wont care and he wont have to deal with those fools anymore. His coat must work if he feels better, because if he's in his room and he feels warmer and happier, than he can walk around naked and not be embarrassed or worry that someone's looking, or have anyone even know what he's doing.

1-Point Response

Its hard to say why or how a song could even be wearing something like a coat since a coat is like a jacket and jackets don't usually go onto songs because they aren't really real. So his song is something like a symbol of something that's ugly and his idea is to put a jacket on it so it'll look better. Or more probably he's going to sing a song somewhere and wants to look nice when he is singing it. People dress up in coats and suits all the time to look better so if he thinks his song is ugly than he can wear coats and suits that will make it look better. People also wear suits for special occasions and meetings too, so maybe he's going to sing a song like at a wedding or graduation or something and needs a nice coat to wear for the occasion so he'll look nice. He finds out that he can make a suit quicker and nicer than the one he can buy in the store, or maybe hes broke and cant even afford to buy one so he just makes it instead. Nice suits are expensive and tuxedos are too. So you rent them. Than he's got a nice suit to where and he thinks everyone else will be jealous cause they are fools and don't know he made the suit himself …it looks that good. He feels better in his suit so his singing is better too. When he comes home he can like relax and walk around naked til he gets into a shower or bath before bed and feel good about the song he sung and all the complements he got for singing and his new suit that he got to wear and show off!

SCORING THE CSET: ENGLISH SUBTEST III

In the English Subtest III, you will respond to two writing prompts. Each provided prompt is designed so that your response essay can be completed in approximately 45–60 minutes.

Your response essays will be scored by California educators using a Focused Holistic Scoring system: *a Focused Holistic Scoring* is a scoring system based on the *overall quality of your writing*, rather than your specific answer to a given prompt. In other words, the people grading your essay response will be looking at your writing fundamentals such as organization and structural continuity, thesis development, syntax, supporting evidence and mechanics, rather than grading your essay(s) as just a topic-related "right" or "wrong" answer. That is, *the scoring committee will be looking at your writing skills* and NOT your correct answer to a given question. Understanding what the graders are looking for gives you the advantage of focusing your time and attention on the overall quality of your writing and frees you from worrying about the "correctness" of your particular answer.

Your essay's grade(s) will be based on a set of standards established by the California Commission on Teacher Credentialing. Consider these already familiar standards as you write your response essay(s).

The Writing Standards or "Performance Characteristics" which the graders will be looking for include:

Purpose: The purpose or extent to which your essay responds only to the given question; that is, not allowing your train-of-thought to get sidetracked or derailed, while addressing the question in a comprehensive and scholarly manner

Subject matter knowledge: Your knowledge of the given subject matter; that is, proving that your knowledge base of the given subject matter meets the CSET subject matter requirements

Support: Your use of appropriate and relevant support materials; that is, your use of significant and/or relevant quotations, data, statistics, and other pertinent evidence

Depth and breadth of understanding: The depth and breadth of your understanding of a given subject; that is, the extent to which your response essay demonstrates your comprehension of the relevant CSET subject matter requirements

These Performance Characteristics will be determined and your essay graded based on the following Scoring Scale (*Grading Rubric*) criteria:

Scoring Scale

4: To earn a four-point (4) score, your response will show that you have a sophisticated grasp of the knowledge and skills (as defined in the subject matter requirements for CSET: English), which include:

- The ability to fully address the purpose of the assignment; that is, your response to the prompt is complete, sophisticated, scholarly, and comprehensive—addressing only the specific prompt without distractions
- The ability to select and include relevant and logical supporting evidence and examples, which demonstrate (and/or represent) your overall understanding of the given subject matter

Ultimately, a four-point (4) essay demonstrates to the committee that you have a comprehensive and complex understanding of the assignment.

3: To earn a three-point (3) score, your response will show the committee that you have an overall or generalized understanding of the knowledge and skills (as defined in the subject matter requirements for CSET: English), which include:

- The ability to recognize and achieve the assignment's large, general, or overall purpose, which in turn demonstrates your overall knowledge of the given subject matter
- The ability to recognize and apply some accurate information and relevant supporting evidence to the given subject matter

Ultimately, a three-point (3) essay demonstrates to the committee that you have an adequate or sufficient understanding of the assignment.

2: To earn a two-point (2) score, your response will show the committee that you have a basic or partial understanding of the knowledge and skills (as defined in the subject matter requirements for CSET: English), which include:

- The ability to achieve the assignment's goals, but only on a limited or partial basis
- The ability to recognize and/or utilize only a minimal amount of relevant subject matter and supporting evidence, based on a limited, myopic, or partial understanding of the CSET sample materials

Ultimately, a two-point (2) essay demonstrates to the committee that you have a limited, narrow-minded, or partial understanding of the assignment.

1:   To earn a one-point (1) score, your response will show the committee that you have little or no understanding of the knowledge and skills (as defined in the subject matter requirements for CSET: English), which include:

- The lack of ability to recognize or achieve the most basic elements and goals of the assignment

- The lack of ability to recognize or apply basic relevant supporting evidence and/or demonstrate little to no understanding of the most basic elements of the CSET sample materials, including how to appropriately respond to them

Ultimately, a one-point (1) essay demonstrates to the committee that you have no adequate or sufficient understanding of the assignment.

U: A grade of "U" (*unable-to-score*) will be given to essays that are completely unrelated to the assignment, illegible, written in a language other than English, and/or which do not contain a sufficient amount of your own original writing. You may notice that some of the problems that cause an essay to earn a "U" are solvable by simply slowing yourself down and pacing yourself as you systematically respond to each question or prompt.

B: A grade of "B" (*blank*) will be given to essay responses left blank. So for heaven's sake, don't ever leave a test question blank if at all possible.

Practice Test 1

Subtest IV –
Communications: Speech, Media, and Creative Performance

This practice test is also on CD-ROM in our special interactive CSET: English TEST*ware*®. It is highly recommended that you first take this exam on computer. You will then have the additional study features and benefits of enforced timed conditions and instant, accurate scoring. See page xvii for instructions on how to get the most out of REA's TEST*ware*®.

Practice Test 1, Subtest IV
Communications: Speech, Media, and Creative Performance

The constructed-response questions that follow are similar to the four questions you will see on Subtest IV of the *CSET: English Test*. Complete each of the exercises without looking at the responses provided in the next section. Record your responses on the sample response sheets and then compare them with the provided responses.

Practice Question 1

To many individuals the terms *public speaking* and *intense stress* are synonymous. Experts have provided us with a wealth of insight and effective measurers to combat these feelings of overwhelming anxiety associated with the act of public speaking.

Write a response in which you

- identify several stress-related symptoms associated with public-speaking anxiety and
- describe the suggested methods of coping with those anxieties.

In your response, be sure to address both of the tasks described above.

Practice Question 2

Discriminating journalists use six basic questions (the five W's and one H) to assemble the facts they will need for an effective article. These six questions (who, what, when, where, why, and how) are important components to any news story, but quality journalism goes beyond answering these six questions and includes an extra responsibility that a reporter has to his or her audience.

Write a response in which you

- briefly describe the idea of quality journalism as it relates to a reporter's responsibility to the audience and
- give an example of the difference between quality (thorough, complete) reporting and superficial (shallow, minimal) reporting.

Practice Question 3

You are a director staging a modern tragedy loosely based on Shakespeare's *King Lear*. The tragic elements of the play demand that your characters build tension, conflict, pathos, and alienation, and ultimately climax in death. As you stage the scene in which the protagonist meets the antagonist for the first time, you'll create the most dramatic tension if you block the characters in which of the following configurations: physically close to one another or standing farther apart from one another?

Select the appropriate response, and explain the theatrical purpose of the effect.

Practice Question 4

Read the following opening paragraph from a preliminary draft of a short story, then complete the exercise that follows.

> On a warm July evening, Bob and Sally perched themselves on a bluff overlooking the placid little bay. The vista was breathtaking, the sunset sublime. The poor unsuspecting couple had no way of knowing that in less than forty-five minutes, the skies over San Diego, California, would be blackened with over a thousand hostile Taiwanese jet fighters, dropping their destructive cargos on the naval ships sleeping gently in their Pearl Harbor berths below.

Using your knowledge of creative writing, write a response in which you

- describe one type of revision you would make to improve the draft excerpt shown above and

- explain why this type of revision would enhance the literary quality of the short story.

English Subtest IV:
Written Response Sample

When you take the CSET: English Test, Subtest IV, you will be given a four-page answer sheet packet, one sheet for each of the four questions. You will have to confine your answer to the lined space provided. You will not write your name on the paper.

Practice writing each of your answers on the following pages.

_____

_____

_____

_____

_____

_____

_____

_____

_____

_____

_____

_____

Written Response Sample Sheets *(cont'd)*

_____

_____

_____

_____

_____

_____

_____

_____

_____

_____

_____

_____

_____

_____

Written Response Sample Sheets *(cont'd)*

Written Response Sample Sheets *(cont'd)*

SAMPLE RESPONSES FOR PRACTICE TEST 1: SUBTEST IV

Question 1

Three-Point Response

For many people, speaking in public is a far worse prospect than death itself. People have reported nervous symptoms ranging from sweaty palms, shaky knees, and cottonmouth, to flu-like symptoms including forgetfulness, heart palpitations, nausea, and even fainting. For nervous individuals facing the prospect of giving an oral presentation, the experts agree, the number one cure is preparation! Be prepared; know your material inside and out, backwards and forwards. While practice makes perfect, preparation precedes practice. So, thorough preparation, planning, and practice are the keys to public speaking success. This preparedness means that you'll present yourself and your material with an air of authority and confidence, as you'll already be secure in the subject you're talking about. Additionally, you will be secure in the knowledge that you'll be able to intelligently respond to any questions or comments that come your way. This confident attitude will not only have a positive effect on the speaker, but on the audience too, as they will accept your presentation more readily.

Two-Point Response

Perhaps it's just human nature that makes people so nervous when they have to give a speech. Some folks can channel that nervous energy into a positive experience, understanding that the extra adrenaline promotes an extra diligence in the construction and presentation of their lecture. For others, it's a nightmare, with the same nightmarish symptoms of heart-pounding fear, jittery paranoia, and head-aching mental breakdowns of forgetfulness, stuttering, and self-hatred.

To combat such symptoms experts recommend everything from slow, deep breathing to picturing the audience in their underwear. Other tactics include putting yourself in the audience and realizing that they want you to do well because nothing is worse than sitting through a boring lecture. You could also focus on people's foreheads instead of their eyes, or you could think positively and visualize yourself successfully completing your talk with nothing but affirmative responses from the audience. What ever techniques you choose to deal with the stress of public speaking, remember the old adage, in 100 years, who's going to care?

One-Point Response

Maybe it's just me, but I hate sitting through a long boring speech. Blah, blah, blah, on and on with nothing to say, it's like time goes backwards. People shouldn't be so monotone and boring when they give speeches. Maybe they wouldn't be so nervous if they just had something interesting to say. I like when a speaker is excited about something their talking about. It's also better for me if the lecture has multimedia to go along with it. I can really understand more about what the speaker is saying when there are also pictures and sounds to go along with it. PowerPoint presentations are really popular now, because you can incorporate slides, video, sound, and music into your presentation and it's all controlled by the person giving the lecture on his laptop. It's a lot more work to put a PowerPoint presentation together, but it's worth it if you have to give the same speech over and over again, and it's more enjoyable to the people that have to listen.

Question 2

Three-Point Response

Quality reporting includes presenting not just the facts pertaining to a particular story or event, but also the direct significance or impact that those facts and events will have on the reader or viewer. So for example, rather than just reporting, "Congress passes constitutional amendment xyz," or "The president vetoes constitutional amendment xyz," a thorough reporter will include the impact or significance that those events will have upon the consumer. The difference is reflected in this rewriting of the two above examples, "Gasoline prices will rise as a result of Congress passing measure xyz," or "The nation's college tuition costs will increase 7% due to the president's veto of measure xyz."

Thus, a minimal journalistic approach will include a presentation of the five W's (who, what, when, where, and why) with the occasional "how" thrown in, but ultimately leaves their audience with the task of deciding what impact the news events will have on them personally. A complete or quality job of reporting, on the other hand, will include the significance or impact that the information had, has, or will have upon the audience.

Two-Point Response

Superficial or careless reporting is commonplace in today's media. It suggests that only the bare minimum of information is reported. So a careless journalist will for example, write an article where he or she critiques a play or performer, i.e. "last night's staging of <u>La Boehme</u> was excellent," "the production value of Gershwin's *Porgy & Bess* is delightful," or "John Doe's acting has never been better," but neglects to include additional pertinent information such as the name of the theater where the show is running, or when the performance times are, or what the tickets cost, etc. All the relevant surrounding information is omitted by the minimalist reporter, or worse, viewed as extraneous information.

The quality reporter will view additional information as relevant and helpful to his/her audience and would include the information omitted in the examples above. The thorough reporter might even add a brief John Doe bio, or they may suggest that Sunday's matinee is less expensive than Sunday night's performance. Whatever it takes, a quality reporter will do the research necessary to bring the complete and thoughtful information package to their audience, including supplementary information to add meaning and purpose to their articles.

One-Point Response

Since writing a good news article isn't brain surgery, it seems that it's up to the reporter to ask what they want to ask, and write whatever they want about a news story, as long as they make sure to include the five or six basic questions. If they don't include all of the basic questions, then they are writing minimal, maybe because they are too lazy or something.

The quality reporter will use a little tape recorder or their cell phone or something so that they can take all the notes exactly right, just like someone said them, rather than just guessing or trying to remember what someone said or what time something happened at, or where something happens, like the subliminal reporter will do. So for an example a lazy reporter will say, I think it happened around 3:15 in the afternoon, and the quality reporter will say, it happened at 3:18 pm, because he wrote it down, or used his cell phone to take a picture and has a record of the exact time.

Question 3

Three-Point Response

To extract the most dramatic tension from a scene, the characters need to be standing farther apart from one another, because the open areas of the stage offer the characters greater opportunities for physical gestures and movements. As a crowded dance floor offers little room to fling one's body around, so too would putting the actors in close proximity to one another, limit their potential for broad physical gestures and movements.

Additionally, characters arranged in close proximity visually suggest a conclusion or resolution to a conflict, like a couple that is physically and emotionally united at the end of a romance. Their close emotional relationship is symbolically represented by their close physical positioning, just as characters in conflict would be staged father apart, with the physical space between them visually representing the emotional space between them. Thus, pulling the characters apart would suggest a physical or emotional separation or tension represented by the empty space between the principle characters and at the same time offers the director and cast greater opportunities for physical and emotional manipulation while it sends visual cues to the audience.

Two-Point 2 Response

It would seem sensible that putting a bigger space between the performers would add more tension to a scene, because the actors would have to project their voices more, and that increased volume in itself would make for more dramatic tension. People "raising their voices" are commonly associated with conflict and tension. Just as the clichéd image of the couple fighting in the restaurant suggests, when one turns to the other and says, "shhh, keep it down, do you want to cause a scene?" So this comment suggests what we already know, people shouting (raising their voices) causes a scene, or in a theatrical sense, infuses a scene with aggression, anger, and/or some form of conflict and tension. The example of the arguing couple also includes the people at the other dinning tables, who are (nervously) trying not to listen to the loud couple. Essentially, the couple's loud voices have a theatrical component built in. The other restaurant patrons are the ones who represent the play's audience. So as a director, I'd want to create the same uncomfortable atmosphere on stage, as the couple arguing in the restaurant causes for the rest of the dinners. By putting a larger space between my principal characters, I can increase the volume of the dialog and thus, increase the tension for the audience.

One-Point Response

If I were the director, I'd be like in your face. I'd put one character right up under the other guy's nose, so that there is the real threat that one guy could swing and hit the other. The audience would worry that a fight was going to break out. One character could push the other one, or stick a finger in the other guy's face, or spit on him, and the audience would be on the edge of their seats. Also, you have to get closer to someone when there's going to be a fight, or no one could reach each other. Also you don't want your main character to look like a wimp and have the audience think he's going to back down, or he's scared and maybe going to run away.

Question 4

Three-Point Response

Even though this is supposed to be a fictional account, it's still important that the author gets their facts right. Factual details solidify characters in a believable time and place, giving both the characters and the storyline more credibility. As there is a national holiday commemorating the infamous event, most Americans know that the attack on Pearl Harbor occurred in the Hawaiian Islands (Oahu), on a December morning (7:00 am, December 7, 1941), not in California on a July evening. Additionally, the attack was instigated by the nation of Japan, not Taiwan. So the characters are in no immediate danger, and the storyline feels juvenile, contrived, and completely unrealistic.

This historical inaccuracy will not only corrupt the believability of the characters and storyline, but will also corrupt the overall tone and timbre of the story. By that I mean that the historical inaccuracies take what could be a suspenseful situation, an unsuspecting couple about to be caught up in a catastrophe, and turn it into a joke, bordering more on the edge of parody or satire, rather than legitimate suspense.

A simple web search or library visit could provide all the fundamental facts and figures necessary to create a believable environment, where the protagonists are in legitimate danger from the impending attack

Two-Point Response

While I'm not exactly sure, I don't think that they had jet fighters in World War II. All the movies I've seen show airplanes with propellers.

While this may not seem like a big deal, it is very distracting for me, since I don't know where or when the story is supposed to be taking place. Maybe the author is trying to update the story. In that case, he/she could add laser beams, space ships, and other high-tech toys. Nevertheless, it is distracting since I'm not sure if the story is supposed to be taking place in the old days when the war really happened or in a fictional "alternate" time and place. Maybe the author is using the events of the Second World War as inspiration only. But regardless of the reason he/she chose, the author should make it clear from the onset, where and when this story actually takes place. That way the reader knows from the start, if they are in an imaginary world or in a real world situation. It would make the story more believable and thematically easier for me to understand.

One-Point Response

Even though I don't know who Bob and Sally are, I think they are going to get married soon. Nothing is more romantic than sitting with your girlfriend by the beach watching the ocean and the sunset. It means he really loves her. If it were me, I'd bring a blanket and wine and something to eat, and some flowers, and we'd sit on a blanket and watch the boats go by. And we'd watch the sunset, and smell the ocean, and listen to the seagulls and the waves, and it would be really romantic. The ocean is really romantic. So it'd be a good place for Bob and Sally to get engaged and maybe even have their wedding there. Then they can go back sometimes, and see where they fell in love and got engaged and it'd be even more romantic for many years. I love going to the beach and playing in the sand and the waves or just sitting on the sand and soak up the sun, or watching all the hot girls in their bikinis. But not if my girlfriend's around. She'd get really jealous. The ocean is a really good spot for a love story.

SCORING THE CSET: ENGLISH SUBTEST IV

In the English Subtest IV, you will respond to four writing prompts. Each provided prompt is designed so that your response essay can be completed in approximately 10–15 minutes.

Your response essays will be scored by California educators using a Focused Holistic Scoring system: *a Focused Holistic Scoring* is a scoring system based on the *overall quality of your writing*, rather than your specific answer to a given prompt. In other words, the people grading your essay response will be looking at your writing fundamentals such as organization and structural continuity, thesis development, syntax, supporting evidence and mechanics, rather than grading your essay(s) as just a topic-related "right" or "wrong" answer. That is, *the scoring committee will be looking at your writing skills* and NOT your correct answer to a given question. Understanding what the graders are looking for gives you the advantage of focusing your time and attention on the overall quality of your writing and frees you from worrying about the "correctness" of your particular answer.

Your essay's grade(s) will be based on a set of standards established by the California Commission on Teacher Credentialing. Consider these already familiar standards as you write your response essay(s).

The Writing Standards or "Performance Characteristics" which the graders will be looking for include:

- The purpose or extent to which your essay responds only to the given question; that is, not allowing your train-of-thought to get sidetracked or derailed, while addressing the question in a comprehensive and scholarly manner

- Your knowledge of the given subject matter; that is, proving that your knowledge base of the given subject matter meets the CSET subject matter requirements

- Your use of appropriate and relevant support materials; that is, your use of significant and/or relevant quotations, data, statistics, and other pertinent evidence.

- The depth and breadth of your understanding of a given subject; that is, the extent to which your response essay demonstrates your comprehension of the relevant CSET subject matter requirements

These Performance Characteristics will be determined and your essay graded based on the following Scoring Scale (*Grading Rubric*) criteria:

To earn a three-point (3) score, your response will show that you have a sophisticated grasp of the knowledge and skills (as defined in the subject matter requirements for CSET: English), which include:

- The ability to fully address the purpose of the assignment; that is, is your response to the prompt complete, sophisticated, scholarly, and comprehensive – addressing only the specific prompt without distractions

- The ability to select and include relevant and logical supporting evidence and examples, which demonstrate (and/or represent) your overall understanding of the given subject matter.

Ultimately, a three-point (3) essay demonstrates to the committee that you have a comprehensive and complex understanding of the assignment.

To earn a two-point (2) score, your response will show the committee that you have an overall or generalized understanding of the knowledge and skills (as defined in the subject matter requirements for CSET: English), which include:

- The ability to recognize and achieve the assignment's large, general, or overall purpose, which in turn demonstrates your overall knowledge of the given subject matter

- The ability to recognize and apply some accurate information and relevant supporting evidence to the given subject matter

Ultimately, a two-point (2) essay demonstrates to the committee that you have an adequate or sufficient understanding of the assignment.

To earn a one-point (1) score, your response will show the committee that you have a basic, partial, or insufficient understanding of the knowledge and skills (as defined in the subject matter requirements for CSET: English), which include:

- The ability to achieve the assignment's goals, but only on a limited or partial basis.

- The ability to recognize and/or utilized only a minimal amount of relevant subject matter and supporting evidence, based on a limited, myopic, or partial understanding of the CSET sample materials.

Ultimately, a one-point (1) essay demonstrates to the committee that you have a limited, narrow-minded, or unsatisfactory understanding of the assignment.

A grade of "U" (*unable-to-score*) will be given to essays that are completely unrelated to the assignment, illegible, written in a language other than English, and/or which do not contain a sufficient amount of your own original writing. You may notice that some of the problems that cause an essay to earn a "U" are solvable by simply slowing yourself down and pacing yourself as you systematically respond to each question or prompt.

A grade of "B" (*blank*) will be given to essay responses left blank. So for heaven's sake, don't ever leave a test question blank if at all possible.

Practice Test 2

Subtest I –
Literature and Textual Analysis;
Composition and Rhetoric

This practice test is also on CD-ROM in our special interactive CSET: English TEST*ware*®. It is highly recommended that you first take this exam on computer. You will then have the additional study features and benefits of enforced timed conditions and instant, accurate scoring. See page xvii for instructions on how to get the most out of REA's TEST*ware*®.

Practice Test 2, Subtest I
Answer Sheet

1. Ⓐ Ⓑ Ⓒ Ⓓ
2. Ⓐ Ⓑ Ⓒ Ⓓ
3. Ⓐ Ⓑ Ⓒ Ⓓ
4. Ⓐ Ⓑ Ⓒ Ⓓ
5. Ⓐ Ⓑ Ⓒ Ⓓ
6. Ⓐ Ⓑ Ⓒ Ⓓ
7. Ⓐ Ⓑ Ⓒ Ⓓ
8. Ⓐ Ⓑ Ⓒ Ⓓ
9. Ⓐ Ⓑ Ⓒ Ⓓ
10. Ⓐ Ⓑ Ⓒ Ⓓ
11. Ⓐ Ⓑ Ⓒ Ⓓ
12. Ⓐ Ⓑ Ⓒ Ⓓ
13. Ⓐ Ⓑ Ⓒ Ⓓ
14. Ⓐ Ⓑ Ⓒ Ⓓ
15. Ⓐ Ⓑ Ⓒ Ⓓ
16. Ⓐ Ⓑ Ⓒ Ⓓ
17. Ⓐ Ⓑ Ⓒ Ⓓ
18. Ⓐ Ⓑ Ⓒ Ⓓ
19. Ⓐ Ⓑ Ⓒ Ⓓ
20. Ⓐ Ⓑ Ⓒ Ⓓ
21. Ⓐ Ⓑ Ⓒ Ⓓ
22. Ⓐ Ⓑ Ⓒ Ⓓ
23. Ⓐ Ⓑ Ⓒ Ⓓ
24. Ⓐ Ⓑ Ⓒ Ⓓ
25. Ⓐ Ⓑ Ⓒ Ⓓ

26. Ⓐ Ⓑ Ⓒ Ⓓ
27. Ⓐ Ⓑ Ⓒ Ⓓ
28. Ⓐ Ⓑ Ⓒ Ⓓ
29. Ⓐ Ⓑ Ⓒ Ⓓ
30. Ⓐ Ⓑ Ⓒ Ⓓ
31. Ⓐ Ⓑ Ⓒ Ⓓ
32. Ⓐ Ⓑ Ⓒ Ⓓ
33. Ⓐ Ⓑ Ⓒ Ⓓ
34. Ⓐ Ⓑ Ⓒ Ⓓ
35. Ⓐ Ⓑ Ⓒ Ⓓ
36. Ⓐ Ⓑ Ⓒ Ⓓ
37. Ⓐ Ⓑ Ⓒ Ⓓ
38. Ⓐ Ⓑ Ⓒ Ⓓ
39. Ⓐ Ⓑ Ⓒ Ⓓ
40. Ⓐ Ⓑ Ⓒ Ⓓ
41. Ⓐ Ⓑ Ⓒ Ⓓ
42. Ⓐ Ⓑ Ⓒ Ⓓ
43. Ⓐ Ⓑ Ⓒ Ⓓ
44. Ⓐ Ⓑ Ⓒ Ⓓ
45. Ⓐ Ⓑ Ⓒ Ⓓ
46. Ⓐ Ⓑ Ⓒ Ⓓ
47. Ⓐ Ⓑ Ⓒ Ⓓ
48. Ⓐ Ⓑ Ⓒ Ⓓ
49. Ⓐ Ⓑ Ⓒ Ⓓ
50. Ⓐ Ⓑ Ⓒ Ⓓ

Practice Test 2, Subtest I
Literature and Textual Analysis; Composition and Rhetoric

1. Paraphrasing is an essential component in the construction of an essay. What is the definition of *paraphrasing*?

    (A) Duplicating the argumentative phrasing twice in strategic locations within the essay

    (B) Restating a text or thesis in your own words thereby making the idea or topic clearer to understand

    (C) Using two parallel symbols to suggest that the argument or textual idea is malleable and therefore subject to scrutiny

    (D) Replacing the author's name with your own, and taking credit for the work that he or she has produced

2. Bede's *Caedmon's Hymn* is one of the first known works of Anglo-Saxon poetry written in the vernacular. What does the phrase *written in the vernacular* mean?

    (A) Written in the everyday language of the people

    (B) Written in Latin

    (C) Written in Old English

    (D) Witten in ink rather than with graphite or carbon

3. *Nothing more and nothing less than the truthful treatment of material* best describes

    (A) literary impressionism.

    (B) literary regionalism.

    (C) literary colonialism.

    (D) literary realism.

4. *Literary naturalism* is best defined as

    (A) a literary attempt to accurately and objectively record visual reality in terms of transient effects of light and color, thereby representing the various shapes and colors found in nature.

    (B) giving the effect that the writing represents the nature of life and the social world as it seems to the common reader.

    (C) the belief that human beings exist entirely in the order of nature and do not have a soul or any participation in a religious or spiritual world beyond nature.

    (D) the representation of the human condition based on loose and free-flowing designs, patterns, and shapes, like those found in nature.

5. The growth of regional literature can be attributed to

    (A) increased popularity of magazines.

    (B) a greater number of female readers.

    (C) a desire to preserve distinct modes of life before industrialization homogenized them.

    (D) all of the above.

6. Which of the following is the title of the autobiography of Booker T. Washington?

    (A) *The Souls of Black Folk*
    (B) *Uncle Tom's Cabin*
    (C) *Yes, I Can*
    (D) *Up from Slavery*

7. Which best describes epic poetry, such as Homer's *The Iliad* and *The Odyssey*?

    (A) An extended narrative poem based upon the heroic exploits and/or extraordinary adventures of an individual involved in an extended quest

    (B) An extended lyrical poem based upon tribal values and religious ideologies of certain indigenous cultures

    (C) An extended prosaic narrative whereby a group of individuals finds spiritual enlightenment through social and spiritual hardship and/or exaggerated strife

    (D) A hyperbolic representation of the feats and actions of a real-life individual who has been characterized for fictional purposes

8. A single-stanza lyric poem consisting of fourteen iambic pentameter lines, ending in a heroic couplet, is better known by what familiar literary term?

    (A) Franciscan or Italian soliloquy

    (B) Petrarchan or Shakespearean sonnet

    (C) English or Anglo-Saxon elegy

    (D) Homeric or Spenserian epistolary

9. Which name from the list below is most closely associated with metaphysical poetry?

    (A) Edmund Spenser

    (B) Robert Herrick

    (C) John Donne

    (D) Alfred Lord Tennyson

Read the following passage, then answer questions 10 to 15.

> SATIRE is a sort of glass wherein beholders do generally discover everybody's face but their own; which is the chief reason for that kind reception it meets with in the world, and that so very few are offended with it. But, if it should happen otherwise, the danger is not great; and I have learned from long experience never to apprehend mischief from those understandings I have been able to provoke: for anger and fury, though they add strength to the sinews of the body, yet are found to relax those of the mind, and to render all its efforts feeble and impotent.
>
> There are but three ways for a man to revenge himself of the censure of the world: to despise it, to return the like, or to endeavor to live so as to avoid it. The first of these is usually pretended, the last is almost impossible; the universal practice is for the second.
>
> A nice man is a man of nasty ideas.
>
> Jonathan Swift

10. Which of the following answers best defines *satire*?

    (A) Satire is a form of ridicule towards social inequities, human vice, and folly as a vehicle to promote social awareness and ultimately positive social change.

    (B) Satire subtly alters the identity of living individuals, but despite these alterations the reader is still expected to recognize the actual person.

    (C) Satire is a form of imitation that pays homage to an actual individual (living or dead) or an actual historical event.

    (D) Satire is a form of scathing intellectual humor that was developed in the Middle Ages and is still in use today.

11. What does Swift mean when he says, "SATIRE is a sort of glass wherein beholders do generally discover everybody's face but their own"?

    (A) Swift means that satire is a vessel that is capable of "holding" or containing social anger and fury.

    (B) Swift means that satire is fragile like glass, and must be "handled" delicately, that is used sensitively, by the satirist.

(C) Swift means that satire exposes human nature, and human nature is such that people "generally" see the flaws in others, but not in themselves.

(D) Swift means that satire is a form of literary "mischief," which ultimately renders or reduces the mind to nothing but feeble and impotent thoughts.

12. What does Swift mean when he declares, "A nice man is a man of nasty ideas"?

(A) Swift suggests that people are basically perverse in their nature and in their thinking, and as a result, spend an inordinate amount of time dwelling on perverted and obscene ideas.

(B) Swift suggests that a nice man is an honest man with honest thoughts, and society, which does not like to hear honest thoughts or ideas, will thus label him nasty.

(C) Swift suggests that society will externally condemn vulgar ideas, but internally supports and condones such ideas and behaviors.

(D) Swift suggests that there is actually no such thing as a nice or decent person, because on the inside, all people are inherently vulgar and debased.

13. In the phrase "the censure of the world," what does *censure* mean?

(A) To edit for appropriate moral content
(B) A device that responds to external stimulus
(C) A moral thought pattern or process
(D) To blame or judge in a sternly condemning manner

14. According to Swift, why is satire "received so kindly" by the world?

   (A) Because everyone needs a good laugh, and satire is essentially a form of humor that everyone enjoys.

   (B) Because satire pokes fun at prominent social figures past and present, and these same social big shots need to be brought down a peg or two.

   (C) Because most people are too ignorant or self-absorbed to understand that the satire is making fun of them.

   (D) Because satire is fresh and contemporary, so the humor doesn't get old or boring like other forms of humor can.

15. What is the overall tone of the Swift treatise?

   (A) Sardonic and sarcastic
   (B) Lighthearted and jocular
   (C) Frivolous and flippant
   (D) Gloomy and dismal

16. Medieval morality plays, *Everyman* being the most famous, are

   (A) dramatized allegories of proper or acceptable domestic behaviors, presented in the plot form of a day in the life of a feudal family.

   (B) dramatized allegories of proper etiquette for commoners who end up in the presence of social superiors and/or royalty.

   (C) dramatized allegories of Christian life, presented in the plot form of a quest for salvation.

   (D) dramatized allegories satirizing improper social behaviors presented in the form of an early *commedia dell'arte*.

17. Literary modernism, seen in works such as T. S. Eliot's *The Waste Land*, is an early twentieth-century style of literature involving which of the following essentials?

    (A) A deliberate and radical attempt to reconnect with romanticized Greco-Roman iconic representations and ideologies, including the use of Latin, ancient Greek, and ancient Hebrew

    (B) A deliberate and conscious attempt to represent the early twentieth century as a period of artistic beauty, social harmony, and historical value

    (C) A deliberate and conscious attempt to avoid early twentieth-century iconic representations, focusing more on the Italian Renaissance period as one of inspiration and social salvation

    (D) A deliberate and radical break with traditional literary conventions by presenting fragmented, opaque, and convoluted images juxtaposed to romanticized classical images and ideologies

18. Sonnets and other forms of English poetry, such as Thomas Gray's "Elegy Written in a Country Churchyard," are written in iambic pentameter. What is iambic pentameter?

    (A) Five lines of poetry with each line consisting of five stressed syllables followed by five light syllables

    (B) Five feet per line of one light syllable followed by a stressed syllable

    (C) A poem limited to five stanzas, with each stanza limited to five lines

    (D) One stressed syllable follow by a light syllable appearing in every fifth word per line

19. Anglo-Saxonic literary works such as *Beowulf* use kennings to enhance literary style and effect. What is a kenning?

    (A) Kennings are archaic forms of medieval allegory used to compensate for the limited vocabulary and education of minstrels, poets, and other oral storytellers.

    (B) Kennings are poetic phrases comprised of figurative language used as descriptive phrases in place of the ordinary name of something.

    (C) Kennings are ambiguous medieval cryptograms that contemporary scholars are still trying to decipher.

    (D) Kennings are extended poems in which a heroic figure embarks upon an extended quest in search of some mythical object or creature.

20. Courtly love is

    (A) a convention of lyric poetry and chivalric romances whereby a lover, usually a bachelor knight, idealizes and suffers agonies on behalf of his unrequited love interest.

    (B) a convention of romance novels and cavalier and metaphysical poetry, whereby a lover, usually an enamored poet, must separate from his love interest, causing him great anguish.

    (C) a convention of pre-medieval and medieval poetry whereby courtesans and others of high ranking social status are instructed on the proper behaviors of the king's court.

    (D) a convention of children's literature that strives to teach proper behaviors and social etiquette for both domestic and social situations.

Read the following paragraph, then answer questions 21 to 24.

> Call me Ishmael. Some years ago—never mind how long precisely—having little or no money in my purse, and nothing particular to interest me on shore, I thought I would sail about a little and see the watery part of the world. It is a way I have of driving off the spleen, and regulating the circulation. Whenever I find myself growing grim about the mouth; whenever it is a damp, drizzly November in my soul; whenever I find myself involuntarily pausing before coffin warehouses, and bringing up the rear of every funeral I meet; and especially whenever my hypos get such an upper hand of me, that it requires a strong moral principle to prevent me from deliberately stepping into the street, and methodically knocking people's hats off—then, I account it high time to get to sea as soon as I can. This is my substitute for pistol and ball. With a philosophical flourish Cato throws himself upon his sword; I quietly take to the ship. There is nothing surprising in this. If they but knew it, almost all men in their degree, some time or other, cherish very nearly the same feelings towards the ocean with me.
>
> Herman Melville, *Moby Dick*, 1851

21. What would you say the overall tone of the paragraph is?

  (A) Slow and/or plodding

  (B) Angry and/or resentful

  (C) Somber and/or melancholy

  (D) Jocular and/or optimistic

22. What does the narrator mean when he says, "This is my substitute for pistol and ball"?

  (A) He means that if he doesn't get to the sea right away, he will kill someone.

  (B) He means that if he must to go to sea one more time, he will kill someone.

  (C) He means that if he must to go to sea one more time, he will kill himself.

  (D) He means that if he doesn't get to the sea right away, he will kill himself.

23. The above paragraph is written in what style?

    (A) Prosaic

    (B) Poetic

    (C) Polymorphic

    (D) Parallel

24. When the narrator refers to "a damp, drizzly November in my soul," he is using what type of figure of speech?

    (A) Simile

    (B) Paradigm

    (C) Trope

    (D) Metaphor

25. The term *alliteration* means which of the following?

    (A) A repetitive vowel sound occurring at the beginning of a word or of a stressed syllable within a word

    (B) A repetitive consonant sound occurring at the beginning of a word or of a stressed syllable within a word

    (C) A repetitive vowel sound occurring at the end of a word or of a stressed syllable within a word

    (D) A repetitive consonant sound occurring at the end of a word or of a stressed syllable within a word

26. What makes concrete poems, also known as *pattern poems*, unique from other, more conventional forms of poetry?

    (A) Concrete poems avoid the use of figurative phrases and ambiguous language, preferring to use symbolic representations that are more literal and thus, concrete.

(B)   Concrete poems are structured around reoccurring refrains or poetic choruses, resulting in a poem that sounds more musical or melodic.

(C)   Concrete poems are poems written in the visual shape of their textual content.

(D)   Concrete poems are poems written at the beginning of the Industrial Revolution, lauding the socio-political benefits of steel and concrete.

27.   From Henry Howard (the Earl of Surrey) to T. S. Eliot and Wallace Stevens, poets have used blank verse for centuries, partially because its natural rhythms replicate those of the English vernacular. What is blank verse?

(A)   Blank verse consists of lines of trochaic hexameter that are unrhymed.

(B)   Blank verse consists of lines of iambic pentameter that are rhymed.

(C)   Blank verse consists of lines of iambic pentameter that are unrhymed.

(D)   Blank verse consists of lines of dactylic heptameter that are rhymed.

28.   When Shakespeare's Richard III first speaks his thoughts aloud or Marlowe's Dr. Faustus mutters an extended expository "meditation," these characters are actually performing a

(A)   cacophony.

(B)   syllogism.

(C)   epiphany.

(D)   soliloquy.

Read the following sonnet, then answer questions 29 and 30.

Shall I compare thee to a summer's day?
Thou art more lovely and more temperate:
Rough winds do shake the darling buds of May,
And summer's lease hath all too short a date:
Sometime too hot the eye of heaven shines,
And often is his gold complexion dimm'd;
And every fair from fair sometime declines,
By chance or nature's changing course untrimm'd;
But thy eternal summer shall not fade
Nor lose possession of that fair thou owest;
Nor shall Death brag thou wander'st in his shade,
When in eternal lines to time thou growest:
So long as men can breathe or eyes can see,
So long lives this and this gives life to thee.

William Shakespeare, *Sonnet XVIII*, 1593–99

29. All sonnets, whether Shakespearean or Petrarchan, contain an heroic couplet. Which two lines in the sonnet above comprise the heroic couplet?

   (A) "So long as men can breathe or eyes can see, / So long lives this and this gives life to thee"

   (B) "Nor lose possession of that fair thou owest; / Nor shall Death brag thou wander'st in his shade"

   (C) "And often is his gold complexion dimm'd; / And every fair from fair sometime declines"

   (D) "By chance or nature's changing course untrimm'd; / But thy eternal summer shall not fade"

30. Which of the following answers best summarizes the theme of Shakespeare's sonnet?

   (A) The metaphors relating to nature suggest that love is a part of nature (a naturally occurring phenomenon of the natural world), and therefore like Nature itself, transcends death, existing eternally.

   (B) The references to "rough winds, untrimm'd," and "Death" suggest a tempestuous theme, one of a love relationship that is both difficult and challenging, but perhaps ultimately worth the effort.

(C)   The narrator's hurried tone and references to the passing of time suggests, like Marvell's enamored plea "To His Coy Mistress," the theme of *carpe diem*, or the need to hurry up and "seize the day" when it comes to love and intimacy.

(D)   The poet's use of extended apostrophe suggests a self-conscious artistic endeavor whereby the theme is one of aesthetic ability rather than the conceptual theme of love and relationships.

Read the following sonnet, then answer questions 31 to 33.

> Loving in truth, and fain in verse my love to show,
> That she (dear She) might take some pleasure of my pain:
> Pleasure might cause her read, reading might make her know,
> Knowledge might pity win, and pity grace obtain;
> I sought fit words to paint the blackest face of woe,
> Studying inventions fine, her wits to entertain:
> Oft turning others' leaves, to see if thence would flow
> Some fresh and fruitful showers upon my sun-burn'd brain.
> But words came halting forth, wanting Invention's stay,
> Invention, Nature's child, fled step-dame Study's blows,
> And others' feet still seem'd but strangers in my way.
> Thus, great with child to speak, and helpless in my throes,
> Biting my truant pen, beating myself for spite—
> "Fool," said my Muse to me, "look in thy heart and write."

Sir Philip Sidney, *Astrophel and Stella*, Canto 1, 1877

31.   This sonnet is an example of either a Petrarchan or a Shakespearean sonnet. Which is it and why?

(A)   It's a Shakespearean sonnet because the structure, style, and tone of the language are definitely seventeenth-century British.

(B)   It's a Shakespearean sonnet because the thematic idea is expanded in three quatrains.

(C)   It's a Petrarchan sonnet because the metaphors and rhyme scheme are of a more classical nature.

(D)   It's a Petrarchan sonnet because the thematic idea is presented in an octave followed by a sestet.

32. When the narrator says, "helpless in my throes," what does he mean by *throes*?

    (A) Spasms of pain; the effects of an upheaval or struggle

    (B) Fits of uncontrollable laughter; a form of hysteria

    (C) Intense feelings of frustration, isolation, and/or loneliness

    (D) Another word for dwellings, rooms, lodgings, and the like

33. When the narrator declares, "great with child to speak," what is he referring to?

    (A) The woman that he loves is pregnant and thus, unobtainable.

    (B) For the poet, reciting his poem is a form of "childbirth."

    (C) Children speak the truth while adults tend to corrupt the truth.

    (D) Pregnancy makes the poet's love interest even more beautiful and desirable.

34. The literary periods known as modern and postmodern first emerged as far back as

    (A) 1822.

    (B) 1558.

    (C) 1922.

    (D) 1776.

35. What is the literary term for a fictional work blending elements of fantasy with ordinary situations, people, and events?

    (A) Metafiction or magical realism

    (B) Nouveau Roman or antinovel

    (C) Social or historical novel

    (D) Gothic romance or prose romance

36. Novels that accentuate elements of medieval castles, dungeons, hidden passages with hidden chambers, and the exploits of a sexually perverse, sadistic villain trying to impose himself upon an innocent young maiden are more commonly referred to as _____ novels.

    (A) grotesque

    (B) episodic

    (C) gothic

    (D) epistolary

37. For the purpose of continuity historians and scholars divide the periods of English literature into various segments. Which of the following puts the segments in the correct chronological order?

    (A) Old English, Middle English, Victorian, Renaissance, neoclassical, romantic, modern

    (B) Old English, Middle English, Renaissance, neoclassical, romantic, Victorian, modern

    (C) Neoclassical, romantic, Victorian, Middle English, Old English, modern, renaissance

    (D) Modern, Victorian, romantic, Neoclassical, Renaissance, Middle English, Old English

38. For the purpose of literary interpretation there are numerous approaches to literary criticism. Which of the terms below are *not* forms of literary criticism?

    (A) Deconstruction, reconstruction, feminist, and Marxist

    (B) New historicism, postcolonial, dialogic, and gendered

    (C) Archetypal, discourse analysis, homophobic, and geriatric

    (D) Reconstruction, new historicism, archetypal, and postcolonial

39. The term that denotes or classifies a recurring type of literature, also called a *literary form*, is more commonly referred to as which of the following?

    (A) Hyperbole

    (B) Syntax

    (C) Zymology

    (D) Genre

40. Every successful college essay needs a clear, coherent thesis. What is a working thesis?

    (A) A single, solidified idea, stated as an assertion, which responds to a question-at-issue.

    (B) A general idea that guides your paper, but an idea that will be refined during the course of your writing.

    (C) A "road map" that guides the reader to the topic and content of the essay.

    (D) An idea that fits the topic, or works well in addressing the assigned question-at-issue.

41. What literary term for a poet's extended meditation to an imaginary person, entity, or personified abstract object is illustrated by the following passage from John Donne's "The Sun Rising"?

    > Busy old fool, unruly Sun
    > Why dost thou thus,
    > Through windows, and through curtains, call on us?

    (A) Onomatopoeia or pragmatism

    (B) Apostrophe or metaphysical conceit

    (C) Personification or figure of speech

    (D) Euphemism or hubris

42. While not in direct competition, seventeenth-century poets such as John Donne and Andrew Marvell coexisted with another "school" of poets including such alumni as Robert Herrick and Ben Jonson. What is the name given to "the Sons of Ben?"

    (A) The Graveyard school of poets

    (B) The Metaphysical school of poets

    (C) The Shakespearean school of poets

    (D) The Cavalier school of poets

43. Robert Herrick's short meditation "Another upon Her Weeping"—"She by the river sat, and sitting there / she wept, and made it deeper by a tear"—is an example of an

    (A) epiphany.

    (B) epic simile.

    (C) elegy.

    (D) epigram.

44. Thomas Gray's "Elegy Written in a Country Churchyard" (1751) is considered by many scholars to be the definitive masterpiece of what school of poets and poetry?

    (A) The Graveyard poets

    (B) The Pre-Raphaelite poets

    (C) The Homeric poets

    (D) The romantic poets

45. In the mid-1800s, English artisans including Dante Gabriel Rossetti and his sister Christina formed a group that attempted to "return to the truthfulness, simplicity, and spirit of art, prior to the early Italian Renaissance." This "brotherhood" is more commonly known as the

    (A) Gregorian poets.

    (B) feudal poets.

    (C) Pre-Raphaelite poets.

    (D) romantic poets.

46. Keats, Shelley (Percy Bysshe and Mary), Coleridge, and Wordsworth are names associated with which period of English literature?

    (A)   The neoclassical period

    (B)   The Victorian period

    (C)   The romantic period

    (D)   The Renaissance period

47. Rather than interpreting a text separated from its historical context, what form of literary criticism deals with texts with respect to their historical and cultural context?

    (A)   New historicism

    (B)   Deconstruction

    (C)   Marxist

    (D)   Poststructuralism

48. Miracle plays, morality plays, and interludes are types of

    (A)   early Edwardian drama, written in a variety of verse and forms.

    (B)   late romantic drama, written in a variety of verse and forms.

    (C)   early contemporary drama, written in a variety of verse and forms.

    (D)   late medieval drama, written in a variety of verse and forms.

49. Samuel Langhorne Clemens, one of the most famous authors in American history, is actually known by a more familiar pen name. What is it?

    (A)   Ambrose Bierce

    (B)   George Eliot

    (C)   Mark Twain

    (D)   Nathaniel Hawthorne

50. At the time he was writing his *Canterbury Tales*, Chaucer would have heard the Great Vowel Shift. During what period of English literature did the Great Vowel Shift and Chaucer's *Canterbury Tales* occur?

    (A) Middle English period

    (B) Old English period

    (C) Renaissance English period

    (D) Commonwealth period

Practice Test 2, Subtest I
Answer Key Chart & Codes

Question	Answer	SMR Code
1	B	1.1 Literary Analysis
2	A	1.2 Literary Elements
3	D	1.3 Literary Criticism
4	C	1.1 Literary Analysis
5	D	1.2 Literary Elements
6	D	1.3 Literary Criticism
7	A	1.1 Literary Analysis
8	B	1.1 Literary Analysis
9	C	1.3 Literary Criticism
10	A	1.2 Literary Elements
11	C	1.2 Literary Elements
12	B	1.3 Literary Criticism
13	D	1.2 Literary Elements
14	C	1.3 Literary Criticism
15	A	1.1 Literary Analysis
16	C	1.2 Literary Elements
17	D	1.2 Literary Elements
18	B	1.2 Literary Elements
19	B	1.2 Literary Elements
20	A	1.2 Literary Elements
21	C	1.1 Literary Analysis
22	D	1.1 Literary Analysis
23	A	1.2 Literary Elements
24	D	1.2 Literary Elements
25	B	1.2 Literary Elements
26	C	1.1 Literary Analysis

Question	Answer	SMR Code
27	C	1.1 Literary Analysis
28	D	1.2 Literary Elements
29	A	1.2 Literary Elements
30	A	1.1 Literary Analysis
31	D	1.1 Literary Analysis
32	A	1.1 Literary Analysis
33	B	1.3 Literary Criticism
34	C	1.3 Literary Criticism
35	A	1.3 Literary Criticism
36	C	1.3 Literary Criticism
37	B	1.3 Literary Criticism
38	C	1.3 Literary Criticism
39	D	1.1 Literary Analysis
40	B	1.2 Literary Elements
41	B	1.2 Literary Elements
42	D	1.1 Literary Analysis
43	D	1.2 Literary Elements
44	A	1.4 Analysis of Non-Literary Texts
45	C	1.4 Analysis of Non-Literary Texts
46	C	1.4 Analysis of Non-Literary Texts
47	A	1.4 Analysis of Non-Literary Texts
48	D	1.4 Analysis of Non-Literary Texts
49	C	1.1 Literary Analysis
50	A	1.4 Analysis of Non-Literary Texts

Practice Test 2, Subtest I Progress Chart: Multiple-Choice Questions

Literary Analysis SMR Code 1.1

1B__ 4C__ 7A__ 8B__ 15A__ 21C__ 22D__ 26C__ 27C__
30A__ 31D__ 32A__ 39D__ 42D__ 49C__   __/15

Literary Elements SMR Code 1.2

2A__ 5D__ 10A__ 11C__ 13D__ 16C__ 17D__ 18B__ 19B__
20A__ 23A__ 24D__ 25B__ 28D__ 29A__ 40B__ 41B__ 43D__   __/18

Literary Criticism SMR Code 1.3

3D__ 6D__ 9C__ 12B__ 14C__ 33B__ 34C__ 35A__ 36C__
37B__ 38C__   __/11

Analysis of Non-Literary Texts SMR Code 1.4

44A__ 45C__ 46C__ 47A__ 48D__ 50A__   __/6

Subtest I (SMR Codes 1.1 to 1.4)   Total __/50

Practice Test 2, Subtest I
Detailed Explanations of Answers

1. **(B)** (SMR 1.1)
   Paraphrasing is restating a text or thesis in your own words thereby making the idea or topic clearer to understand for both the writer and the reader.

2. **(A)** (SMR 1.2)
   Caedmon's Hymn was written in the everyday language of the people. Up until the time of Bede, most literature was written in Latin or other non-vernacular language.

3. **(D)** (SMR 1.3)
   Realism was a nineteenth-century literary movement attempting to replicate everyday life situations as realistically as possible. The works of authors William Dean Howells and Hamlin Garland are representative of American realism.

4. **(C)** (SMR 1.1)
   Literary naturalism is the belief that human beings exist entirely in the order of nature and do not have a soul or any participation in a religious or spiritual world beyond nature. Staged in an indifferent, deterministic universe, naturalistic texts "often describe the futile attempts of human beings to exercise free will in a universe that reveals free will as an illusion."

5. **(D)** (SMR 1.2)
   Regional literature or local color is fiction and poetry that focus on the characters, dialect, customs, topography, and other features particular to a specific region.

6. **(D)** (SMR 1.3)
   There are strong ideological differences between W. E. B. Du Bois's *Souls of Black Folk* (1902) and Booker T. Washington's *Up from Slavery* (1901). These two texts established lasting battle lines on a variety of major issues dealing with racial identity and civil rights in the United States.

7. **(A)** (SMR 1.1)
   An *epic poem* is an extended narrative poem based upon the heroic exploits and/or extraordinary adventures of an individual involved in an extended quest. The hero is usually a male character, capable of superhuman feats, who performs in a way that reflects and lauds the *central beliefs* and *culture* of his society.

8. **(B)** (SMR 1.1)
    Petrarchan or Italian sonnets are named after the fourteenth-century Italian poet Francesco Petrarch, while sixteenth-century refinements evolved into the Shakespearean or English sonnets.

9. **(C)** (SMR 1.3)
    John Dryden said in his Discourse of Satire (1693) that John Donne's poetry "affects the metaphysics," meaning in a sense, that Donne epitomized and/or set the standards for this abstract, intellectualized, and idealized style of poetry.

10. **(A)** (SMR 1.2)
    Satire is a form of imitative ridicule with a subject matter that focuses on social inequities and human corruption.

11. **(C)** (SMR 1.2)
    People see the hypocrisy in others but seldom see it in themselves.

12. **(B)** (SMR 1.3)
    In this case Swift is using the adjective *nice* as a euphemism for *honest*, and by doing so he suggests that society will demonize honesty by labeling it as something "nasty."

13. **(D)** (SMR 1.2)
    In the quote *censure* means to blame or judge in a sternly condemning manner.

14. **(C)** (SMR 1.3)
    Swift's trademark scathing commentary suggests that people are too ignorant or self-absorbed to understand that the humor is representative of and directed at them.

15. **(A)** (SMR 1.1)
    Swift, maybe better than any other writer, uses sardonic wit and sarcasm to ridicule in order to expose social vice and folly.

16. **(C)** (SMR 1.2)
    Morality plays dramatize early Christian principles and precepts, graphically showing the final punishment for not following Christian doctrine.

17. **(D)** (SMR 1.2)
    Modernism is a deliberate and radical attempt by early twentieth-century artists to break from traditional artistic conventions by presenting fragmented, opaque, eclectic, and convoluted images juxtaposed to romanticized classical images and ideologies.

18. **(B)** (SMR 1.2)

    Used in a variety of English poetry forms including blank verse, sonnets, heroic couplets, and so on, iambic pentameter is five feet per line of one light syllable followed by a stressed syllable.

19. **(B)** (SMR 1.2)

    Kennings, such as *whale-road* (ocean) and *ring-giver* (king), are poetic phrases comprised of figurative language used as descriptive phrases in place of the ordinary name of something.

20. **(A)** (SMR 1.2)

    Courtly love is a staple of lyric poems and chivalric romances whereby a lover, usually a bachelor knight suffers great agonies and moral victories on behalf of his (usually) unrequited or unobtainable love interest.

21. **(C)** (SMR 1.1)

    Phrases such as "growing grim about the mouth" and "a damp, drizzly November in my soul" establish the passage's somber and melancholy tone.

22. **(D)** (SMR 1.1)

    The narrator means that if he doesn't get to the sea right away, he will kill himself. In other words, it suggests that sailing is the only cure for his depression.

23. **(A)** (SMR 1.2)

    The paragraph is written in a prosaic style, that is, having the characteristics of a prose narrative, as opposed to a poetic style and structure.

24. **(D)** (SMR 1.2)

    "A damp, drizzly November in my soul" is a metaphor, whereby symbols replace literal representations.

25. **(B)** (SMR 1.2)

    Alliteration is the repetition of a consonant sound occurring at the beginning of a word or of a stressed syllable within a word, as in *Peter Piper picked a peck of pickled peppers*, or *She sells sea shells by the sea shore.*

26. **(C)** (SMR 1.1)

    Concrete or pattern poems use a visual shape to present their content, such as a poem about a goblet written in the shape of a drinking glass, or George Herbert's "Easter Wings" and "The Altar."

27. **(C)** (SMR 1.1)

    Blank verse, first solidified by the Henry Howard around 1540, consists of poetic lines of iambic pentameter (five-stress iambic verse) that are unrhymed, hence the term *blank*. This structure allows for the flexibility to replicate natural speech patterns and the adaptability to accommodate diverse subject matters.

28. **(D)** (SMR 1.2)

    A soliloquy is an action in a performance whereby the character on stage speaks his or her thoughts to the audience, perhaps providing necessary plot information, personal motives, general exposition, and so forth.

29. **(A)** (SMR 1.2)

    Both English and Italian sonnet structures require the heroic couplet (lines of iambic pentameter that rhyme in pairs: *aa*, *bb*, *cc*, etc.) to appear at the end of the stanza.

30. **(A)** (SMR 1.1)

    The sonnet is saturated with metaphors of nature from "summer days" to flower "buds" in "May," intertwined with images of "life" and "death." As the presumably male narrator extends his contemplations, he realizes that as long as people "live," "see," and "breathe," his affection will too.

31. **(D)** (SMR 1.1)

    A Petrarchan sonnet, such as the opening canto from Sidney's Astrophel [Astrophil] and Stella, presents the thematic idea in two main parts. The first is the octave (eight lines), which contemplates an idea, conflict, or issue; the second is a sestet (six lines), which attempts to resolve the idea, conflict, or issue.

32. **(A)** (SMR 1.1)

    A throe is a spasm of pain or the effect of an upheaval or struggle. Here the love-smitten narrator suffers over his desire for a lady that is not his social equal and therefore is unobtainable.

33. **(B)** (SMR 1.3)

    Poets often equate the act of creating a poem with that of giving birth to a child.

34. **(C)** (SMR 1.3)

    While some scholars consider the onset of the modern period to extend as far back as the 1860s, it is generally accepted that it began in earnest right after World War I ended, circa 1922.

35. **(A)** (SMR 1.3)

The prose fiction of authors like Gabriel García Márquez combines the extraordinary elements of fantasy and mundane elements of reality and is known as magical realism, or metafiction.

36. **(C)** (SMR 1.3)

Gothic novels, such as Horace Walpole's *The Castle of Otronto* (1764), emerged in the later part of the eighteenth century and are still a popular form of literary entertainment today.

37. **(B)** (SMR 1.3)

Old English, Middle English, Renaissance, Neoclassical, Romantic, Victorian, Modern periods.

38. **(C)** (SMR 1.3)

While archetypal and discourse analysis are legitimate forms of literary criticisms, homophobic (having an irrational fear and hatred of homosexuals) and geriatric (relating to the health care of the elderly) are not accepted forms of literary criticisms.

39. **(D)** (SMR 1.1)

Genre is a word of French origin, which denotes the categorizing or classification of literary works by subject. Genres can include but are not limited to such categories as westerns, science fiction, horror, mystery, and detective stories.

40. **(B)** (SMR 1.2)

A working thesis, as opposed to a finished or final thesis, is a general idea of the direction your essay will take, but one that will ultimately be refined and clarified as your essay develops.

41. **(B)** (SMR 1.2)

The excerpt is an example of an apostrophe or metaphysical conceit.

42. **(D)** (SMR 1.1)

The Cavalier poets, including the likes of Robert Herrick, Thomas Carew, and Richard Lovelace, wrote in polished, lyrical, erotically charged poems of gallantry and courtship.

43. **(D)** (SMR 1.2)

An epigram is any very short poem (whether meditative, elegiac, satirist, anecdotal, etc.) that is elegant, concise, and usually ends with a witty or pointed turn of thought.

44. **(A)** (SMR 1.4)

The Graveyard poets were a group of eighteenth-century poets—Thomas Gray, Edward Young, and Thomas Parnell—who wrote meditative poems usually set and/or written in a cemetery, contemplating the happenstances of life and death.

45. **(C)** (SMR 1.4)

The pre-Raphaelites were a brotherhood of poets who attempted to return to the ideals of truthfulness, simplicity, and art prior to the Italian Renaissance.

46. **(C)** (SMR 1.4)

The authors are all associated with the romantic period.

47. **(A)** (SMR 1.4)

New historicism deals with texts with respect to their historical and cultural context.

48. **(D)** (SMR 1.4)

Miracle plays, morality plays, and interludes typify late-medieval drama.

49. **(C)** (SMR 1.1)

Mark Twain was the pen name for Samuel Langhorne Clemens, who took his pen name from the language of the river boats he so loved.

50. **(A)** (SMR 1.4)

The Middle English period saw the occurrence of the Great Vowel Shift and also served as the setting for Chaucer's *Canterbury Tales*.

Practice Test 2

Subtest II –
Language, Linguistics, and Literacy

This practice test is also on CD-ROM in our special interactive CSET: English TEST*ware*®. It is highly recommended that you first take this exam on computer. You will then have the additional study features and benefits of enforced timed conditions and instant, accurate scoring. See page xvii for instructions on how to get the most out of REA's TEST*ware*®.

Practice Test 2, Subtest II
Answer Sheet

1. Ⓐ Ⓑ Ⓒ Ⓓ
2. Ⓐ Ⓑ Ⓒ Ⓓ
3. Ⓐ Ⓑ Ⓒ Ⓓ
4. Ⓐ Ⓑ Ⓒ Ⓓ
5. Ⓐ Ⓑ Ⓒ Ⓓ
6. Ⓐ Ⓑ Ⓒ Ⓓ
7. Ⓐ Ⓑ Ⓒ Ⓓ
8. Ⓐ Ⓑ Ⓒ Ⓓ
9. Ⓐ Ⓑ Ⓒ Ⓓ
10. Ⓐ Ⓑ Ⓒ Ⓓ
11. Ⓐ Ⓑ Ⓒ Ⓓ
12. Ⓐ Ⓑ Ⓒ Ⓓ
13. Ⓐ Ⓑ Ⓒ Ⓓ
14. Ⓐ Ⓑ Ⓒ Ⓓ
15. Ⓐ Ⓑ Ⓒ Ⓓ
16. Ⓐ Ⓑ Ⓒ Ⓓ
17. Ⓐ Ⓑ Ⓒ Ⓓ
18. Ⓐ Ⓑ Ⓒ Ⓓ
19. Ⓐ Ⓑ Ⓒ Ⓓ
20. Ⓐ Ⓑ Ⓒ Ⓓ
21. Ⓐ Ⓑ Ⓒ Ⓓ
22. Ⓐ Ⓑ Ⓒ Ⓓ
23. Ⓐ Ⓑ Ⓒ Ⓓ
24. Ⓐ Ⓑ Ⓒ Ⓓ
25. Ⓐ Ⓑ Ⓒ Ⓓ

26. Ⓐ Ⓑ Ⓒ Ⓓ
27. Ⓐ Ⓑ Ⓒ Ⓓ
28. Ⓐ Ⓑ Ⓒ Ⓓ
29. Ⓐ Ⓑ Ⓒ Ⓓ
30. Ⓐ Ⓑ Ⓒ Ⓓ
31. Ⓐ Ⓑ Ⓒ Ⓓ
32. Ⓐ Ⓑ Ⓒ Ⓓ
33. Ⓐ Ⓑ Ⓒ Ⓓ
34. Ⓐ Ⓑ Ⓒ Ⓓ
35. Ⓐ Ⓑ Ⓒ Ⓓ
36. Ⓐ Ⓑ Ⓒ Ⓓ
37. Ⓐ Ⓑ Ⓒ Ⓓ
38. Ⓐ Ⓑ Ⓒ Ⓓ
39. Ⓐ Ⓑ Ⓒ Ⓓ
40. Ⓐ Ⓑ Ⓒ Ⓓ
41. Ⓐ Ⓑ Ⓒ Ⓓ
42. Ⓐ Ⓑ Ⓒ Ⓓ
43. Ⓐ Ⓑ Ⓒ Ⓓ
44. Ⓐ Ⓑ Ⓒ Ⓓ
45. Ⓐ Ⓑ Ⓒ Ⓓ
46. Ⓐ Ⓑ Ⓒ Ⓓ
47. Ⓐ Ⓑ Ⓒ Ⓓ
48. Ⓐ Ⓑ Ⓒ Ⓓ
49. Ⓐ Ⓑ Ⓒ Ⓓ
50. Ⓐ Ⓑ Ⓒ Ⓓ

Practice Test 2, Subtest II
Language, Linguistics, and Literacy

1. According to United Nations Educational, Scientific, and Cultural Organization census figures, as of April 2006, worldwide adult illiteracy had reached

   (A) 781 million adults.

   (B) 427 million adults.

   (C) 100 million adults.

   (D) 1 billion adults.

2. A good working definition for the term *literacy* is found in *Read to Succeed*, from the Kentucky Literacy Partnership (June 2002). Which answer below best fits the working definition of *literacy*?

   (A) *Literacy* includes the ability to read and enjoy printed materials in a variety of forms, such as magazines, books, and newspapers.

   (B) *Literacy* includes reading, writing, and the creative ability to produce works of literary art.

   (C) *Literacy* includes the ability to write (articulate) your thoughts in a variety of formats including printed forms, diaries, journals, and so forth.

   (D) *Literacy* includes anyone over the age of eighteen who can read and write correctly.

3. While the figures vary, the general consensus is that nearly one-third of the American adult population is functionally illiterate. Which of the following best describes someone who is functionally illiterate?

   (A) One who is limited to the ability of correctly writing his or her own name

   (B) One who is able but reluctant to read or write in his or her native language

   (C) One who is able to read and write in his or her native language, but with only the most rudimentary degree of *grammatical* skills and comprehension

   (D) One who must use a dictionary or other reference source to comprehend reading materials

4. A fundamental definition of the term *language* is

   (A) the use of symbols or pictographs (symbols representing words) as a system of communication.

   (B) the use of auditory sounds that are recognized by another as a representational or symbolic system of communication.

   (C) the repetitious use of hand gestures as a system of communication.

   (D) the use of spoken or written words as a system of communication.

5. According to the Child Development Institute, what is the average age at which children begin to recognize and respond to their own name?

   (A) Six months
   (B) Two months
   (C) Eight months
   (D) Twelve months

6. What does the word *echolalia* mean?

    (A) The advanced formation of words based upon their root word

    (B) The repetitious speaking of words spoken by someone else

    (C) The ability to hear the alliterative properties of a word

    (D) The ability to recognize similar sounding morphemes

7. According to a 1998 language acquisition study conducted by Cornell University, "human babies are born with the ability to

    (A) visualize symbolic concepts."

    (B) comprehend tonal inflections as well as visual cues."

    (C) develop positive or negative language skills and abilities, based solely on external stimuli, such as environment."

    (D) grasp the complex rules of word order and sentence structure in any language."

8. If linguistics is the study of language, then what is applied linguistics?

    (A) The study of language anomalies with regard to gender, age, and nationality

    (B) The study of language components in a physical, biological, or anatomical sense

    (C) The study of language as it relates to practical or real-world communication issues

    (D) The study of language application, ranging from guttural expletives to sophisticated repartee

9. The study of linguistics would include which of the following?

   (A) Studying the relationship of languages, including the variations and similarities that all oral or written languages share

   (B) Studying the nature, structure, and development of language(s), indigenous and foreign, including language origins and the development of alphabets and written languages

   (C) Studying the organizational patterns of both foreign and domestic languages, including phonetic and emblematic representations

   (D) Studying the specific vocal and physiological apparatuses of speech and speech patterns, including the auditory apparatuses related to hearing and comprehension

10. The term *literacy partnership* refers to which of the following?

    (A) A combined effort on the part of local and national schools, families, and communities to eradicate illiteracy

    (B) A combined effort on the part of local and national government agencies targeting the eradication of illiteracy

    (C) A combined effort on the part of local and national institutions to eradicate illiteracy by providing reading materials such as textbooks to economically depressed communities

    (D) A combined national and international grassroots effort to spread information on the devastating socioeconomic effects of living with illiteracy

11. Native speakers who do not speak the same language are sometimes able to communicate through a simplified language made up of the elements of two or more languages; this simplified language is more commonly known as

    (A) lingua franca.

    (B) phonetics.

(C) pidgin.

(D) euphony.

12. The Center for Applied Linguistics, assessment standards, and common sense agree that the basic principle of a language acquisition program should be which of the following?

(A) A program of instruction that stresses the commonalities in languages, thereby making the transition from one language to the next phonetically simpler

(B) A program of instruction that tests students' natural language aptitudes and tailors a customized curriculum based on the particular students' abilities and weaknesses

(C) A program of instruction that puts students at ease with the process of language acquisition

(D) A program of instruction that challenges all students academically and linguistically

13. What is a mother tongue?

(A) The language skills acquired from the maternal (mother's) side of the family

(B) The first language a person learns, that is, their native language

(C) The accepted language of the area or region where a person lives

(D) The Latin base from which our modern-day languages developed

14. A noun formed from a verb by the addition of -ing, as in swim to swimming, is known as a

(A) gerund.

(B) apostrophe.

(C) anecdote.

(D) genre.

15. Identify the two parts that make up the following topic sentence: *Cultural anthropology courses teach that different cultures solve the same problems in different ways.*

    (A) The predicate: *Cultural anthropology courses*;and the thesis: *teach different cultures*

    (B) The noun: *Cultural anthropology*; and the topic: *teach* [about] *different cultures*

    (C) The topic: *Cultural anthropology courses*; and the claim: [they] *teach . . . different cultures*

    (D) The claim: *cultures solve the same problems*; and the topos: *different cultures . . . different ways*

16. When two independent clauses are not joined correctly, the sentence is known as a

    (A) fragmented sentence.

    (B) topic sentence.

    (C) run-on sentence.

    (D) comma splice sentence.

17. What is a compound verb?

    (A) A compound verb consists of two or more verbs connected by a conjunction such as *and*, *but*, or *or*.

    (B) A compound verb is a verb that adds *-ly* to the end, as is *easy* to *easily*.

    (C) A compound verb is a verb that functions as both noun and verb, as in *I was at the lake,* **fishing**.

    (D) A compound verb is a verb supported by adverbs, as in *very upset*.

18. In the sentence *Pull gently on an old rope*, the word *gently* is a(n)

    (A) noun.

    (B) verb.

    (C) adjective.

    (D) adverb.

19. What must a sentence contain in order for it to be considered a complete sentence?

    (A) A predicate and a claim

    (B) A noun and a verb

    (C) A verb and an adjective

    (D) A noun and an adjective

20. What is the definition of a *paragraph*?

    (A) A group of sentences that develop the various aspects of certain ideas or claims.

    (B) A group of sentences that express the author's emotional response to an issue.

    (C) A group of sentences that develop one main (complete) idea.

    (D) A group of sentences that express the contemporary views of a society.

21. In the phrase *to boldly go where no man has gone before*, what is the grammatical term for *to boldly go*?

    (A) Hyperbolic paradigm

    (B) Compound verb

    (C) Grammatically correct

    (D) Split infinitive

22. When a writer chooses between words like *was/were*, *have/had/has*, or *run/ran*, he or she is actually selecting the appropriate

    (A) gendered nouns.

    (B) extraneous adjectives.

    (C) proper nouns.

    (D) verb tense.

23. What is the more common term for "a word used to modify, or qualify a verb, an adjective, or another adverb"?

    (A) Adverb

    (B) Noun

    (C) Adjective

    (D) Verb

24. What is the difference between a linking verb and a helping verb?

    (A) A linking verb substitutes for a conjunctive, as in *hit and run*, while a helping verb establishes verbal intensity, as in *he was mad* versus *he was very mad*.

    (B) A linking verb renames or describes the subject, while a helping verb augments information about the main or essential verb.

    (C) A linking verb "links" a verb phrase with a noun phrase, while helping verbs "help" establish the parallel relationship between the noun and the verb.

    (D) A linking verb is another name for an adverb or adverb phrase, while a helping verb simply substitutes for an adjective or adjectival phrase.

25. Identify the problem in the following sentence: *I was on my way to the store for some supplies when my tire goes flat.*

    (A) The sentence contains a dangling participle.

    (B) The sentence has no clear referent and is thus a sentence fragment.

    (C) The sentence contains an incorrect verb-tense agreement.

    (D) Inappropriate punctuation results in a comma splice.

26. The term *etymology* can be defined as

    (A) the study of a word's origins, including its history and evolution.

    (B) the study of a word's origins, including its meaning in a cultural context.

    (C) the study of a word's history, including its relationship to another word.

    (D) the study of the era in which a word entered the language.

27. Scholars use philology to study ancient codices and other noncontemporary texts. What is philology?

    (A) The study of language universality regardless of social context

    (B) The study of language in its cultural and social context

    (C) The study of all literary prose in a contextual context

    (D) The study of alphabets, symbols, and primitive written languages

28. According to various sources on the improvement of literacy skills, in order to stimulate children's imagination, parents and teachers should take the time to

    (A) read aloud to children.

    (B) model positive reading habits.

    (C) encourage children to read beyond their grade level.

    (D) encourage children to read rather than watch TV or play video games.

29. When a student has difficulty with reading retention, the recommended procedure for improving retention skills would include

    (A) using classroom materials designated for lower grade levels; these are less intimidating.

    (B) increasing the amount of time the student spends on repetition and review.

    (C) reading aloud, slowly and clearly, articulating as many words as possible.

    (D) designating the child as developmentally disabled and referring him or her to counseling.

30. Studies comparing three decades of long-term reading assessment data found that there is a direct connection between increased illiteracy and

    (A) a decrease in vocabulary skills.
    (B) the intellectual ability of the modern reader.
    (C) the decline of reading materials in the home.
    (D) school inabilities to support an overcrowded population.

31. In 1999, a long-term assessment study by the National Assessment of Educational Programs found a positive relationship between children's reading scores and

    (A) the economic income level of their parents.
    (B) the social standings of their parents.
    (C) the ethnic origins of their parents.
    (D) the educational level of their parents.

32. Phonetics, the study of the sounds of human language; phonology (or phonemics), the study of patterns of a language's basic sounds; and morphology, the study of the internal structure of words all belong to the category of

    (A) applied linguistics.
    (B) advanced technology.

(C) applied sciences.

(D) humanities.

33. A word that shares phonetic similarities with another word, as in *sea* and *see*, is more commonly known as a(n)

(A) acronym.

(B) dictaphone.

(C) homophone.

(D) synonym.

34. In a typical language development situation, a four-year-old child should be able to

(A) tell time and relate complex information about events that happened in the past.

(B) name familiar animals and common objects in picture books, newspapers, or magazines.

(C) comprehend simple instructions, especially when accompanied by vocal and/or physical cues.

(D) articulate the relationship between a photograph and an abstract idea.

35. A vocabulary of five to twenty words comprised mostly of nouns is characterisitic of a typically developing child of approximately what age?

(A) Eighteen months

(B) Four years

(C) Six months

(D) Six years

36. When incorporating the use of computers and other technology into your preschool or kindergarten lesson plans, two important questions need to be considered. What are the two questions?

   (A) Is the technology cost effective; that is, does it pay to utilize the technology in terms of school revenue and teacher time investment? And will that revenue be offset in future returns such as taxes and school bonds?

   (B) Is the technology developmentally appropriate; that is, is the technology consistent with the children's developmental stage? And will the activity benefit the children, or will it replace some other, more meaningful learning activities?

   (C) Are the positive benefits of the technology enough to outweigh the negative aspects of overexposing young children to technology, and how will that overexposure manifest itself in our society when these same children reach maturity?

   (D) Is the technology consistent with the overall academic environment, or is it simply an electronic babysitter for the classroom? And does it provide teachers with more teaching methods and tools, or is technology removing accountability from educators?

37. Basic adult reading skills might include

   (A) reading calendar dates, labels, flyers, brochures, and newspaper classifieds.

   (B) reading manuals, graphs, charts, spreadsheets, diagrams, and blueprints.

   (C) reading sporadically and randomly, whether for information or enjoyment.

   (D) reading a variety of media with focus and purpose.

38. Which of the following best defines *hermeneutics*?

    (A) A branch of linguistics that focuses on the explanation and interpretation of ancient Greco-Roman scrolls and manuscripts

    (B) A branch of science that focuses on the explanation and interpretation of modern and postmodern texts

    (C) A branch of language arts that focuses on the explanation and interpretation of legal documents and legal jargons

    (D) A branch of theology that focuses on the explanation and interpretation of codices and scripture

39. Which of the following is the best example of onomatopoeia?

    (A) Ha-ha, whip, hop, hope
    (B) Sneeze, cough, laugh, blink
    (C) Buzz, hiss, whoosh, ding-dong
    (D) Zip, bump, jump, stump

40. Which of the following sentences contains a dangling modifier?

    (A) Maria watched TV all night long.
    (B) Last night, I shot an elephant in my pajamas.
    (C) Jake had no idea which direction to choose.
    (D) Keiko wanted dinner, but her brother Elmo wasn't hungry yet.

41. *Carpe diem* is a characteristic commonly associated with what type of poetry?

    (A) Cavalier
    (B) Post-Modern
    (C) Metaphysical
    (D) Elegiac

42. Which of the following definitions best represents *guttural speech*?

    (A) A phrase containing vulgar or taboo language, usually employed for the purpose of degrading or offending the listener

    (B) A series of phonetic sounds produced in the avuncular region of the throat.

    (C) A short burst of air, produced by the contraction of muscles in the stomach or gut region

    (D) A harsh, raspy, or grating sound produced in the back of the mouth or throat

43. When people adopt a pidgin as their primary language, and it becomes the mother tongue of a community, the pidgin transforms into a(n)

    (A) indigenous.
    (B) ambiguous.
    (C) Creole.
    (D) dialect.

44. The more common name for a lexicon is

    (A) an encyclopedia.
    (B) a dictionary.
    (C) a catalog.
    (D) a textbook.

45. Cryptology, also known as *cryptography*, is the study and analysis of

    (A) coded, secret, or encrypted languages.
    (B) cave drawings and archeological markings.
    (C) markings found exclusively in crypts and ancient tombs.
    (D) primate sounds.

46. A drawing used to represent an entire word or an idea is called a(n)

    (A) apostrophe.

    (B) pictograph.

    (C) metaphor.

    (D) allusion.

47. What is cuneiform script?

    (A) A phonetic form of writing, adaptable to the sounds of any language

    (B) A hybrid script blending hieroglyphs and modern alphanumeric symbols

    (C) The world's earliest known forms of written language

    (D) A primitive form of writing developed by Native Americans

48. The discovery of the Rosetta Stone in 1799 was an incredible find for both archeologists and linguists alike. Why?

    (A) Since the stone is a black basalt stone, it did not deteriorate over time as other materials do, enabling translators to easily read the text printed on the stone.

    (B) Since the stone is Mesopotamian, historians and philologists now know that the world's earliest written languages come from Istanbul and Turkey.

    (C) Since the stone was found on a battlefield, it provided important clues regarding ancient tribal battles and the world's earliest known military strategies.

    (D) Since the stone is imprinted with the same text written in two ancient languages, translators were able to decipher previously unreadable Egyptian hieroglyphs.

49. While the term *morphology* can pertain to a field of biological study, it is also a branch of linguistic study. What is morphology?

    (A) Morphology is the study of the fundamental structure and formation of words including inflection, derivation, and the formation of compound words.

    (B) Morphology is the study of an indigenous culture's ability to assimilate or adapt various sounds and vocal patterns into their own vocabulary.

    (C) Morphology is the study of ancient tablets, codices, and scrolls for the purpose of understanding the evolution of language over extended periods of time.

    (D) Morphology is the study of the ancient scribes who crafted alphabets and translated text for the illiterate, as they provided "modern" writing structures and fundamentals still in use today.

50. The origin for our modern English language is

    (A) Latin.
    (B) Greek.
    (C) Germanic.
    (D) Roman.

Practice Test 2, Subtest II
Answer Key Chart & Codes

Question	Answer	SMR Code
1	A	2.3 Literacy Studies
2	A	2.3 Literacy Studies
3	C	2.3 Literacy Studies
4	D	2.1 Human Language Structures
5	A	2.1 Human Language Structures
6	B	2.2 Acquisition & Development of Language & Literacy
7	D	2.1 Human Language Structures
8	C	2.2 Acquisition & Development of Language & Literacy
9	B	2.2 Acquisition & Development of Language & Literacy
10	A	2.2 Acquisition & Development of Language & Literacy
11	C	2.2 Acquisition & Development of Language & Literacy
12	D	2.3 Literacy Studies
13	B	2.2 Acquisition & Development of Language & Literacy
14	A	2.4 Grammatical Structures of English
15	C	2.4 Grammatical Structures of English
16	C	2.4 Grammatical Structures of English
17	A	2.1 Human Language Structures
18	D	2.4 Grammatical Structures of English
19	B	2.4 Grammatical Structures of English
20	C	2.1 Human Language Structures
21	D	2.4 Grammatical Structures of English
22	D	2.4 Grammatical Structures of English
23	A	2.4 Grammatical Structures of English
24	B	2.4 Grammatical Structures of English

Question	Answer	SMR Code
25	C	2.4 Grammatical Structures of English
26	A	2.3 Literacy Studies
27	B	2.3 Literacy Studies
28	A	2.2 Acquisition & Development of Language & Literacy
29	B	2.3 Literacy Studies
30	C	2.3 Literacy Studies
31	D	2.2 Acquisition & Development of Language & Literacy
32	A	2.3 Literacy Studies
33	C	2.1 Human Language Structures
34	B	2.2 Acquisition & Development of Language & Literacy
35	A	2.3 Literacy Studies
36	B	2.2 Acquisition & Development of Language & Literacy
37	A	2.2 Acquisition & Development of Language & Literacy
38	D	2.1 Human Language Structures
39	C	2.1 Human Language Structures
40	B	2.4 Grammatical Structures of English
41	A	2.1 Human Language Structures
42	D	2.1 Human Language Structures
43	C	2.1 Human Language Structures
44	B	2.4 Grammatical Structures of English
45	A	2.1 Human Language Structures
46	B	2.3 Literacy Studies
47	C	2.1 Human Language Structures
48	D	2.1 Human Language Structures
49	A	2.1 Human Language Structures
50	C	2.3 Literacy Studies

Practice Test 2, Subtest II
Progress Chart:
Multiple-Choice Questions

Human Language Structures SMR Code 2.1

4D__ 5A__ 7D__ 17A__ 20C__ 33C__ 38D__ 39C__
41A__ 42D__ 43C__ 45A__ 47C__ 48D__ 49A__   __/15

Acquisition & Development of Language & Literacy SMR Code 2.2

6B__ 8C__ 9B__ 10A__ 11C__ 13B__ 28A__ 31D__ 34B__
36B__ 37A__   __/11

Literacy Studies SMR Code 2.3

1A__ 2A__ 3C__ 12D__ 26A__ 27B__ 29B__ 30C__ 32A__
35A__ 46B__ 50C__   __/12

Grammatical Structures of English SMR Code 2.4

14A__ 15C__ 16C__ 18D__ 19B__ 21D__ 22D__ 23A__
24B__ 25C__ 40B__ 44B__   __/12

Subtest II (SMR Codes 2.1 to 2.4)   Total __/50

Practice Test 2, Subtest II
Detailed Explanations of Answers

1. **(A)** (SMR 2.3)
   Worldwide, 781 million adults are illiterate.

2. **(A)** (SMR 2.3)
   Literacy includes not only the acts of reading and writing but the analytical skills required to comprehend (analyze) and produce a form of written text. That is, literacy is not just forming vocal sounds correctly, it's also understanding what is being said, read, and/or written.

3. **(C)** (SMR 2.3)
   Functionally illiterate refers to those who are capable of reading and writing in their native language, but with only the most rudimentary degree of *grammatical* and comprehension skills. These same people cannot perform fundamental tasks such as filling out applications or following written instructions, reading a *newspaper* or street signs, or consulting a *dictionary*, map, and/or *bus* schedule.

4. **(D)** (SMR 2.1)
   Language is an abstract concept, so defining it is the equivalent of defining God or love. For the purposes of the CSET, however, you can approach the definition of language from a linguistic or scientific perspective. Generally speaking, then, a language is our (human) ability to express and comprehend our abstract needs, desires, morals, values, beliefs, and so forth through written and oral communication.

5. **(A)** (SMR 2.1)
   Research shows that by six months of age, a child will recognize and respond to his or her name. In addition, a child at this age will respond to various tonal inflections, such as a happy tone or angry tone, without the need for visual cues.

6. **(B)** (SMR 2.2)
   Echolalia is the repetitious speaking of words spoken by someone else. In adults this compulsion could signal a psychiatric disorder, but in toddlers of approximately eighteen months, it is a positive sign of language development.

7. **(D)** (SMR 2.1)
According to cognitive psycholinguist Barbara Lust, "Our studies show that both American and Taiwanese children as young as 3 years of age already possess a remarkable knowledge of language structure and syntax which is so complex and precise that it must challenge any known learning theory to account for its acquisition."

8. **(C)** (SMR 2.2)
Applied linguistics is the study of language as it relates to practical or real-world communication issues. Such issues might include the acquisition and development of foreign language(s), speech therapy, specialized occupational languages and related communication problems such as the translation of legal jargon, and so on.

9. **(B)** (SMR 2.2)
Linguistics is the systematic study of language, including the components that constitute language in all their various forms.

10. **(A)** (SMR 2.2)
While illiteracy does impact our society in a plethora of negative ways, the term literacy partnership relates to the current combined efforts on the part of local and national schools, communities, and families to eradicate illiteracy.

11. **(C)** (SMR 2.2)
Usually used in commerce, pidgin (or "contact language") is a language composed of various simplified elements of other languages for the purposes of communication.

12. **(D)** (SMR 2.3)
Whether students are learning a single language or multiple languages, the language acquisition program in which they are engaged must challenge them both academically and linguistically.

13. **(B)** (SMR 2.2)
One's mother tongue is one's indigenous or native language, that is, the first language one learns to speak.

14. **(A)** (SMR 2.4)
A gerund is formed by adding *-ing* to a verb, resulting in a word that functions as a noun. For example, a verb like *swim* or *ski* becomes the name of the activity itself: He enjoys swimming, but skiing is his favorite sport.

15. **(C)** (SMR 2.4)

    A topic sentence comprises two parts: a topic and a claim.

16. **(C)** (SMR 2.4)

    A run-on sentence is a sentence in which two or more independent clauses have been run together without a conjunction or proper punctuation.

17. **(A)** (SMR 2.1)

    A compound verb consists of two or more verbs that are connected by a conjunction (and, but, or) and that have the same subject, as in José walked to school and took the big test.

18. **(D)** (SMR 2.4)

    An adverb is a word that modifies a verb, an adjective, or another adverb. In the sentence *Pull gently on an old rope*, the adverb gently modifies the verb *pull*.

19. **(B)** (SMR 2.4)

    A complete sentence must have a noun and a verb.

20. **(C)** (SMR 2.1)

    A paragraph is a group of sentences that develop one main idea.

21. **(D)** (SMR 2.4)

    Infinitives—a verb plus the word *to*, as in *to go*, *to do*, and *to be*—avoid reference to time and thus are considered "infinite." For example, the sentence, "I am going to go to the store," could mean, "I'm on my way to the store now," or it could mean, "I will be going to the store some undesignated time in the future." A split infinitive is an infinitive in which an adverb or other modifier separates the to from the verb, as in to boldly go.

22. **(D)** (SMR 2.4)

    Verb tense indicates the relationship between the action and the time the action takes or took place, as in, "I swam earlier this morning" [past tense]; "I am swimming now" [present tense]; "I will swim tonight" [future tense].

23. **(A)** (SMR 2.4)

    As stated earlier, an adverb modifies a verb, adjective, or another adverb.

24. **(B)** (SMR 2.4)

Linking verbs do not show action; they connect or "link" the subject to something that renames or describes the subject, as in the sentence, "Sarah is a genius," where the subject *Sarah* is linked to a noun that is, in a sense, standing in for her: *genius*. Helping verbs "help" the main verb express time or ask a question, as in, "Lorraine and Arthur have been dancing for decades," where *have been* orients or "helps" the verb *dancing* establish longevity.

25. **(C)** (SMR 2.4)

There is an incorrect verb-tense agreement between the past-tense *was* (I was on my way) and the present tense *goes* (when my tire goes flat). Since the tire and I were both going to the store at the same time, the action occurring to both of us must agree, and as such, the corrected sentence would say, "I was on my way to the store . . . when the tire went flat."

26. **(A)** (SMR 2.3)

Etymology is the study of a word's origins, including its history and evolution. Etymology offers a fascinating perspective from which to view the living aspects of a language's development and growth.

27. **(B)** (SMR 2.3)

Philology is the study of a language in its cultural and social context.

28. **(A)** (SMR 2.2)

Reading aloud to children not only presents a good reading role model, but it also augments attention span and listening skills while nurturing emotional development.

29. **(B)** (SMR 2.3)

Increase the amount of time the student spends on repetition and review. Generally speaking, your lesson plans should include more time for repetition and review than you'd consider necessary.

30. **(C)** (SMR 2.3)

Studies have documented the connection between an increase in illiteracy and a decline of diverse forms of reading materials in the home.

31. **(D)** (SMR 2.2)

The long-term assessment study found that at all three ages (9, 13, and 17), "Children with parents who had some education after high school had the highest reading scores."

32. **(A)** (SMR 2.3)
Phonetics, phonology, and morphology all fall within the scope of applied linguistics.

33. **(C)** (SMR 2.1)
A homophone or homonym is a word that is pronounced the same way as another word, but has a different meaning and/or spelling, as in *two*, *to*, and *too*.

34. **(B)** (SMR 2.2)
A four-year-old child should be able to name familiar animals and common objects in picture books, in addition to knowing one or more colors and most if not all of the vowel sounds.

35. **(A)** (SMR 2.3)
By the age of eighteen months, a typical child should have a vocabulary of approximately five to twenty words, mostly nouns, along with the ability to follow simple commands.

36. **(B)** (SMR 2.2)
The questions to ask are "Is the technology developmentally appropriate, and will the activity benefit the child, or will it replace some other, more meaningful learning activities?" Technology is already an integral part of the classroom and is primarily just another set of teaching tools from which the teacher can choose.

37. **(A)** (SMR 2.2)
Basic adult reading skills include the ability to read and comprehend dates on a calendar; labels on food, clothing, and household products; and flyers, brochures, and newspaper classifieds.

38. **(D)** (SMR 2.1)
Hermeneutics is the science of interpreting texts, especially those pertaining to scripture and codices.

39. **(C)** (SMR 2.1)
Onomatopoeia nouns are words that imitate or mimic the sound they represent, as in *buzz*, *hiss*, *whoosh*, and *ding-dong*, answer (C).

40. **(B)** (SMR 2.4)

    A dangling modifier is a word or phrase that modifies a word not clearly stated in the sentence. A modifier describes, clarifies, or gives more detail about a concept, and should appear next to the words or idea it modifies. The dangling modifier in answer (B) is the prepositional phrase *in my pajamas*, which is supposed to modify *I* but appears to be modifying *elephant*. The corrected sentence would say, "Last night, while wearing my pajamas, I shot an elephant."

41. **(A)** (SMR 2.1)

    A common motif in Cavalier poetry is carpe diem (meaning "seize the day"). Its thematic representation is usually eroticized, employing both wit and elegant, lyrical language.

42. **(D)** (SMR 2.1)

    Guttural speech is characterized by harsh, raspy, or grating sounds produced in the back of the mouth or throat. It is usually associated with languages having Germanic, French, and Semitic origins.

43. **(C)** (SMR 2.1)

    A Creole is a unique language of mixed origin, which has taken most of its vocabulary from another language but has its own unique grammatical rules.

44. **(B)** (SMR 2.4)

    A lexicon is a dictionary. The word's origins stem from Greek, where its original meaning was "vocabulary."

45. **(A)** (SMR 2.1)

    Cryptology, also called cryptography, is the study and analysis of coded, secret, or encrypted languages.

46. **(B)** (SMR 2.3)

    A pictograph is a graphic symbol or picture used to represent an entire word or idea, as opposed to a letter of the alphabet, which represents an individual sound.

47. **(C)** (SMR 2.1)

    Cuneiform, created by the Sumerians over five thousand years ago, is the world's earliest known form of written language. It remained in use up to approximately 75 AD.

48. **(D)** (SMR 2.1)

The Rosetta Stone is imprinted with the same text written in two ancient languages, Egyptian hieroglyphs and ancient Greek, thus providing historians and translators with the key to understanding and deciphering previously unreadable Egyptian hieroglyphs.

49. **(A)** (SMR 2.1)

Morphology is the study of the fundamental structure and formation of words including inflection, derivation, and the formation of compound words.

50. **(C)** (SMR 2.3)

While English is a compilation of many languages, primarily it's Germanic in origins.

Practice Test 2

Subtest III – Composition and Rhetoric; Literature and Textual Analysis

This practice test is also on CD-ROM in our special interactive CSET: English TEST*ware*®. It is highly recommended that you first take this exam on computer. You will then have the additional study features and benefits of enforced timed conditions and instant, accurate scoring. See page xvii for instructions on how to get the most out of REA's TEST*ware*®.

Practice Test 2, Subtest III Composition and Rhetoric

Practice Question 1

Write a critical essay in which you analyze the following selections, supporting your conclusions with specific evidence from the texts. Assume that you are writing for an educated audience knowledgeable about literary criticism. In your essay:

- identify a significant theme that the two texts share;

- compare and contrast the writer's two perspectives on the theme you have identified;

- examine how the writer uses literary techniques, including genre features, literary elements, and rhetorical devices, to express his perspectives on this theme in each piece; and

- draw a conclusion that explains how the literary techniques you have identified affect the ideas conveyed in the texts.

"THE CHIMNEY SWEEPER"

William Blake, *Songs on Innocence*, 1789

When my mother died I was very young,
And my father sold me while yet my tongue
Could scarcely cry 'weep! 'weep! 'weep! 'weep!'
So your chimneys I sweep, and in soot I sleep.

There's little Tom Dacre, who cried when his head,
That curled like a lamb's back, was shaved: so I said,
"Hush, Tom! never mind it, for when your head's bare,
You know that the soot cannot spoil your white hair."

And so he was quiet; and that very night,
As Tom was a-sleeping, he had such a sight, -
That thousands of sweepers, Dick, Joe, Ned, and Jack,
Were all of them locked up in coffins of black.

And by came an angel who had a bright key,
And he opened the coffins and set them all free;
Then down a green plain leaping, laughing, they run,
And wash in a river, and shine in the sun.

Then naked and white, all their bags left behind,
They rise upon clouds and sport in the wind;
And the angel told Tom, if he'd be a good boy,
He'd have God for his father, and never want joy.

And so Tom awoke; and we rose in the dark,
And got with our bags and our brushes to work.
Though the morning was cold, Tom was happy and warm;
So if all do their duty they need not fear harm.

"THE CHIMNEY SWEEPER"
William Blake, *Songs of Experience*, 1794

A little black thing in the snow,
Crying "weep! weep!" in notes of woe!
"Where are thy father and mother? Say!"—
"They are both gone up to the church to pray.

"Because I was happy upon the heath,
And smiled among the winter's snow,
They clothed me in the clothes of death,
And taught me to sing the notes of woe.

"And because I am happy and dance and sing,
They think they have done me no injury,
And are gone to praise God and his priest and king,
Who make up a heaven of our misery.

Practice Question 2

Write a critical essay analyzing the excerpt below from Ralph Waldo Emerson's *Essays*. Assume that you are writing for an educated audience, and make sure to support your conclusions with evidence from the text. In your essay

- summarize, in your own words, the author's main argument in this passage;
- evaluate the author's reasoning;
- describe the author's methods of persuasion and use of rhetorical devices;
- identify the audience for which the author is most likely writing; and
- describe the extent to which the passage is likely to be effective in persuading this audience, and explain why.

Our age is retrospective. It builds the sepulchers of the fathers. It writes biographies, histories, and criticism. The foregoing generations beheld God and nature face to face; we, through their eyes. Why should not we also enjoy an original relation to the universe? Why should not we have a poetry and philosophy of insight and not of tradition, and a religion by revelation to us, and not the history of theirs? Embosomed for a season in nature, whose floods of life stream around and through us, and invite us by the powers they supply, to action proportioned to nature, why should we grope among the dry bones of the past, or put the living generation into masquerade out of its faded wardrobe? The sun shines to-day also. There is more wool and flax in the fields. There are new lands, new men, new thoughts. Let us demand our own works and laws and worship.

Ralph Waldo Emerson, "Nature," 1836

English Subtest III: Written Response Sample

When you take the CSET: English Test, Subtest III, you will be given a four-page answer packet to use for each of the questions. You will have to confine your answer to the lined space provided. You will not write your name on the paper.

Practice writing one of your answers on the following pages.

_____

_____

_____

_____

_____

_____

_____

_____

_____

_____

_____

Written Response Sample Sheets *(cont'd)*

Written Response Sample Sheets *(cont'd)*

_____

_____

_____

_____

_____

_____

_____

_____

_____

_____

_____

_____

_____

_____

Written Response Sample Sheets *(cont'd)*

SAMPLE ESSAYS FOR PRACTICE TEST 2: SUBTEST III

Sample Response for Practice Question 1

Four-Point Response

In both versions of William Blake's "The Chimney Sweeper," contiguous images of a lonely child's misery, isolation, and suffering represent the Victorian philosophy that children are industrial commodities to be exploited and discarded when they are of no further use.

In both poems, a prepubescent or pubescent orphaned narrator voices his misery with sounds of "weeping." His crying is instigated in both versions first, as a result of the loss or abandonment of his parents, "my mother died … and my father sold me …" and "father and mother … both gone to the church to pray," and secondly by the harsh and hazardous labor, the "chimneys I sweep," he is obligated to perform. Additionally, the fact that the narrator is consciously aware that his father "sold" him addresses the issue of Victorian children as a viable commodity. Thus, the opening lines of both versions establish images of an isolated, suffering, exploited child-narrator.

Simultaneously, images of death permeate both poems. In version 1, death is manifested in "coffins of black," while in version 2 the "little black thing" is actually wearing "the clothes of death." These referential images create a dark, "cold," brooding atmosphere reinforcing the fact that the narrator, who sleeps "in soot," exists in a blackened world fraught with suffering and mortal danger, allowing little to no chance for repose.

While both versions suggest a heavenly redemption of sorts, whereby "God" and "angels" will watch the "thousands of happy [adolescent] sweepers leaping, laughing, running, sing[ing] and danc[ing], down a green plain," the fact that both poems end with the words "harm" and "misery" implies a hollow belief or misplaced trust in this impending redemption.

Overall, the poetic references to an orphaned, weeping child "sold" into a world of perpetual darkness and death reinforce the poems overall thematic ideas of a Victorian child's fragile and vulnerable commoditization, resulting in perpetual melancholy and eventually death.

Three-Point Response

"Tom Dacre cries, Dick, Joe, Ned, and Jack [are] all locked in coffins," and a nameless narrator "weep[s] notes of woe!" These images of identified children along with the "thousands" more who remain unnamed, suggests a "cold, black" world where the joys of adolescent innocence are replaced with the harsh laborious conditions of an industrialized 19th-century England. And while England's industrialization produced radical life changes for the better, the history of child labor and child exploitation demonstrates the negative social affects of industrialization.

The proliferation of "chimney's" for example, appearing in both poems, produce an image of a city abundant with factory "soot" (i.e. pollution), and industrial byproducts. The two poems juxtapose images of the environment along side the "weeping" children to suggest that a), the children are a natural resource also being exploited by industrialization, and b), that the city's fragile environment, i.e. "clouds, rivers, wind, sun, snow," is in jeopardy of destruction and thus, unavailable for future generations.

Overall, the references to "weeping, woe, misery, injury, [and] death," apply to both the individual children's suffering as well as the environment's potential to suffer the same "miserable" and deadly fate.

The second version of the poem refers specifically to "churches, God, priests [and] kings" because these are the only ones with enough power to change the course of London's environmental future, as shown in the last line where "a heaven," on earth perhaps, can be made "of our misery."

Two-Point Response

Well, it almost seems like these are just the same poems. Both made me really sad. I don't like the idea of little children "suffering" or dead. Why would Blake write about kids this way? Why are they going to work in the "cold and dark" instead of the daytime?

It says Tom is "a good boy" and yet it seems that he would rather play in the "river" and "in the sun." but instead he has to go to work. Maybe Blake is telling us that work is good for kids. Maybe he wants us to know that without a good day's work the kids won't appreciate their free time as much. They can laugh and play "in the snow" after the work is done. It's really telling us good work values and ethics, since all kids like to play more than they like to work. They are little "angels" who need their moms and dads to support them and give them the love and guidance like all parents give their children. If "Tom" sleeps when the other kids go to work, than maybe he's saying that he's lazy and that lazy is bad while hard work is good. It teaches kids responsibility for when they are adults. I don't think they should be "naked" though when they play. That isn't really teaching them good values like the work ethic part of the poems is.

I think Blake is telling us in these poems that hard work is good for kids and that they need to be taught good work ethics and values so they can grow up to be good people like their parents who pray and believe in God. "God, churches, and angels" are in both of these poems because God is a good influence in the life of children and adults and God says that idle hands are the devil's playground, so that the kids won't be just wasting their time playing games all day like they do now, but will be busy working hard and believing in God so they are learning good values for when they grow up and become adults.

One-Point Response

Both these two poems are really boring and stupid. If the people don't like their jobs they can just quit and get another one. I had a boss once who was really mean and one day he was mean and rude to me in front of the customers so I told him that it wasn't nice to talk to me like that in front of the customers and he said that I was fired, so I quit and then a week later I got another job making stuffed bears at the mall. It wasn't hard, I just walked in and asked if they needed somebody and they said come back on Thursday and I got the job. So why doesn't Mr. Blake quit his job if isn't happy? He could just not go to work and instead go out and find another job. It's not hard making stuffed toys but sometimes it gets really busy and then we get all rushed but I take my time and do a good job on each one I make.

Sometimes bosses can be mean but some can be nice. I had one boss once who was really nice and he liked the way I put the decorations in the window so he made me in charge of decorating the windows and he said I did a really good job. Once he even said that I made the display look like a Macy's store window and I got embarrassed and laughed because I thought he was making fun of me until he told me that that was a good thing. So I got to do the store windows and one year at Christmas, I brought my friends over to see the windows I decorated and they all really liked it a lot and said it was really cool and I felt really good. So if Mr. Blake didn't like his job or his boss was really mean or rude to him or he just didn't like what he was doing then he could just quit and find a new job instead of complaining like he does in the poems.

Also he could ask his parents for help because parents are supposed to help their kids when they are in trouble or need money and such so why doesn't Mr. Blake just ask his parents for money? If he is a little kid than maybe he could do chores around the house or maybe he could mow lawns for the neighbors of something like that to earn extra money. You could get a paper route or something but then he'd have to get up early every morning and do it everyday even Christmas and New Year's day. But that's ok because my little brother did that until he got enough money for a new bike he wanted and he liked it even more because he got to earn it himself. Maybe Mr. Blake is so sad because he doesn't know how good it'd be for him to earn his own money and get what he wanted by working hard; but if his boss is just too mean or whatever than he should just quit going to his chimney job and find something else that he'd like to do better.

Sample Essays for Practice Question 2

Four-Point Response

Emerson's essay uses a series of rhetorical questions to develop his thesis that a modern generation need not carry the antiquated precepts and beliefs of former generations into the modern era. Rather, Emerson suggests that "we" develop our own artistic representations "poetry," religious ideology, and intellectual "philosophy of insights" based on nineteenth-century issues and ideologies rather than simply maintaining the outdated beliefs of former generations.

Emerson crafts an effective argument by presenting a series of logical, thought-provoking questions targeted at a literary audience who cannot respond to the speaker directly and thus is forced to grapple with the answers to these questions internally.

His logic is based on the assertion that "our age is retrospective," and there is little to no room for the reader to refute this premise since there is little debate that "we [indeed do] ... write biographies, histories, and criticism[s]."

While our biblical ancestors "beheld God and nature face to face," it is less likely that a modern contemporary will be able to do the same, unless we understand that Emerson's iconic word choice, i.e. "God" "sepulchers," and "revelation," is suggesting that the modern intellectual transcend or see beyond the faith-based physical relationship mankind once had to "God and nature" and accept these images as metaphors for a contemporary and intellectualized philosophy of belief and spirit.

The essay successfully achieves its goal of intellectual stimulation as it proposes a modern-day "philosophical" revolution of sorts, whereby scholars will cast out the antiquated "revelations" of former generations, and accept the contemporary ideologies of the "insight[ful]" nineteenth-century intellectuals, such as Emerson himself.

Three-Point Response

Emerson's *Essay* explores the idea that the social beliefs or values of our "ancestors" are not necessarily the beliefs or values of the early nineteenth-century society. For example, when Emerson suggests that "our age" (the 19th-century) "builds the sepulchers of our fathers" (ancestors), he is presenting a two-fold argument, in the form of a double-entendre. First, the language proposes the idea that modern society builds monuments to ancestors which both embellish and glorify their archaic achievements. Secondly, the reference to "sepulchers," a synonym for "tombs" places these same "fathers" in a "dead" environment; an environment no longer of "philosophical" or practical social value to a modern generation.

This double-entendre works as the basis for Emerson's argument, which is that while "we" may need to maintain these ancestral icons of the past, as those who do not learn from the past are destine to repeat it, at the same time understanding that our modern generation needs to establish their own viable philosophies and artistic representations based on contemporary needs, beliefs, and understandings and not those of bygone generations.

Emerson is of course successful in the presentation of his concepts, because he leaves little room for a counterargument. The facts he presents are irrefutable since a), he presents them in the form of rhetorical (unanswerable) questions, which are actually simply statements of fact presented in the form of a question, and b) since they are facts, i.e. former generations based their understanding of "the universe" on their direct perceptions," they are not open to debate.

By using this rhetorical structure for his essay, Emerson success-fully sets us the syllogistic premise that if you as an enlightened or intellectual reader accept the facts as he presents them, than you must accept his logical conclusion based on those facts as well. In a bit of an ironic twist then, Emerson is using classical Aristotelian rhetori-cal principles to present his progressive ideas on the establishment of new social ideologies.

Two-Point Response

In the Emerson excerpt above, we see that Emerson doesn't agree with the idea that we can learn and grow from our "fathers" ideas. He thinks they are outdated, and useless. It seems like he's suggesting that there is little to no value in accepting the "philosophies and in-sights" of former generations.

But this is a one-sided argument, since there is much to be learned from "our fathers." The bible tells us, for example that "our fathers" talked to "God, face to face," so how or why would we question this di-rect authority? Since, according to Emerson, we no longer talk directly to God, where is this modern day "revelation" going to come from? By not addressing the answers to the questions he asks, Emerson gives the reader "dry bones" as bits of emotionally charged but highly incom-plete thoughts based on the idea that the ancients have nothing of value or substance to offer a modern "philosopher."

Emerson wants us to adopt "new ways to worship," but fails to address what's wrong with the "old" ways other than proclaiming that they are "old." It is this very antiquity that to some make these forms of worship seem outdated, while to others it's this very connection with our elders that makes these forms of worship meaningful. Refer-ring to the past as a pile of "dry bones," lets us know that Emerson doesn't see any "meat" or substance in the past, but he fails to ad-dress the idea that for many, the past is a source of comfort and inspiration.

Essentially, by not addressing the rational counterarguments, Emerson is trying to persuade a modern reader by coercion (in this case, coercion through emotionally charged language), rather than by a logical series of point-by-point ideas and counter-ideas.

One-Point Response

Emerson's *Nature* essay seems to me to be more about religion than it is about Nature. I mean Sunshine, streams, and floods are parts of nature but I don't really see what they have to do with God and worship and all. Unless he means that God made the floods and the fields and all. I guess maybe that's what he means when he says he demands his own laws to worship. Why doesn't Emerson just go to another church if he doesn't like the one he's in?

Part of what's so hard to understand is his language that he uses. He uses lots of big words that are hard to understand and they really don't make any sense but they do make the essay really hard and boring to understand. He could just have used regular words to say what he wanted to say and then the whole thing would be easier to understand. So for me it was hard to understand what he wanted me to know, and he sounds stupid because no one really talks like that or uses words like that anymore.

I guess he means that maybe like when you have a friend and she gets married outside rather than in a church, like my friend who got married in her aunt's garden last spring, that it's like bringing the church outside into nature and than you can have religion along with nature. Like she had her bouquet made up of all the flowers in her aunt's garden and then the bride's maids dresses were the colors of the flowers in the garden and decorated with the flowers from her actual garden, and the minister wore a flower from her garden on his jacket, so its like Emerson was saying that you can have flowers in church or church in your flowers.

So maybe a "sepulcher" is like a church or a garden or something where they decorate it with lots of flowers and crosses and holy water and people go there to pray. Than they can be praying to god and still smell the flowers and see god's bounty and think about how beautiful the garden is thanks to god. Maybe Emerson is saying then that the gardens and the world is beautiful thanks to God and we should be thankful too to god for the flowers and gardens and our fathers who love us.

Practice Test 2

Subtest IV –
Communications: Speech, Media, and Creative Performance

This practice test is also on CD-ROM in our special interactive CSET: English TEST*ware*®. It is highly recommended that you first take this exam on computer. You will then have the additional study features and benefits of enforced timed conditions and instant, accurate scoring. See page xvii for instructions on how to get the most out of REA's TEST*ware*®.

Practice Test 2, Subtest IV
Communications: Speech, Media, and Creative Performance

The constructed-response questions that follow are similar to the questions you will see on Subtest IV of the CSET: English. Complete of the exercises without looking at the responses provided in the next section. Record your responses on a sheet of paper and then compare them with the provided responses.

Practice Question 1

Why is maintaining eye contact with your audience such an important component of an effective oral presentation?

Write a response in which you

- identify two positive elements of maintaining direct eye contact with an audience and

- describe a negative outcome of not maintaining direct eye contact during a speech or oral presentation.

In your response, be sure to address both of the tasks described above.

Practice Question 2

Why must a reporter maintain a neutral tone of voice and never editorialize (express personal opinions) when relating a news story?

Write a response in which you

- name a negative consequence of editorializing and
- describe how remaining objective adds to the reporter's credibility.

Practice Question 3

When a stage director wants to focus the audience's attention on a particular character or object, he or she can either place the character or object in motion or use a shift in lighting to create the same effect.

Explain why this technique of motion is such an effective directing tool, and describe what happens when more than one object is moving simultaneously.

Practice Question 4

Read the following opening paragraph from a preliminary draft of a short story, then complete the exercise that follows.

> Dayton said he wanted to go to the movies, but Stella would have nothing to do with it and she abruptly told him so to his face. He was pretty ruffled by her response, as he hadn't expected such an outburst on a special night like this. But he said nothing and kept his outward cool all right. Inside, however, he was shaken to his core. Dayton wondered why Stella would say those awful things to him, tonight, of all nights, on his birthday!

Using your knowledge of creative writing, write a response in which you

- describe one type of revision you would make to improve the draft excerpt shown above, and

- explain why this type of revision would enhance the literary quality of the short story.

English Subtest IV: Written Response Sample

When you take the CSET: English Test, Subtest IV, you will be given a four-page answer sheet packet, one sheet for each of the four questions. You will have to confine your answer to the lined space provided. You will not write your name on the paper.

Practice writing each of your answers on the following pages.

_____

_____

_____

_____

_____

_____

_____

_____

_____

_____

_____

Written Response Sample Sheets *(cont'd)*

Written Response Sample Sheets *(cont'd)*

Written Response Sample Sheets *(cont'd)*

SAMPLE RESPONSES FOR PRACTICE TEST 2: SUBTEST IV

Question 1

Three-Point Response

Eye contact with an audience is a critical component of effective speaking because it lets the audience know the speaker is interested in them as individuals rather than as a collective group. If the speaker shows a genuine interest in the audience, it is more likely that the audience will respond in kind, by showing a more genuine interest in the materials being presented. Conversely, a speaker who avoids eye contact with the audience appears lethargic and perhaps worse, apathetic, leaving the audience to respond with the same perceived boredom and indifference. Changed "your/you" to objective articles "a/an"

Direct eye contact with an audience also conveys the speaker's knowledge of and confidence in the materials that they are presenting. A speaker's lack of familiarity with or comprehension of the material(s) they are presenting will reflect in their eyes, as a less confident speaker will be more likely to avoid eye contact with the audience by nervously shifting their gaze from one random vantage point to another. On the other hand, a confident speaker who is well versed in the material(s) being presented will make direct eye contact with as many audience members as possible.

Two-Point Response

With direct eye contact you can let the audience know that you are there for them. You want them to know that you are there to share your information with them and that you like what you're talking about. If you can talk about a topic that you're really interested in than you can tell about it with more enthusiasm and that enthusiasm comes through in your eyes. So for the listeners, the speech seems more exciting and engaging if the speaker looks at them directly in the eyes, rather than just looking at their note pages or at the back of the room, or even worse yet, the clock on the wall.

Since the listeners will be more involved if the speaker looks at them directly, the speech will seem interactive and not tedious. Time won't drag on for the speaker or the listener. Nothing is worse than a lackluster lecture where the topic is dull and the orator is mentally bored else. Time drags when instead of looking at their audience with excitement, the speaker is looking off into someplace they'd rather be, and this shows in their eyes.

One-Point Response

Eye contact is important because it means that you like talking to people. Some people like talking to people and some don't. So, if you do, you'll look at them. It makes a big difference if you look at someone or not. Even in school or with friends you should look at people when you talk to them. It's just courteous. It lets people know that you're polite and have good manners. Good manners are important wherever you go, and it doesn't matter if you're at home or giving a speech you should still be polite and give people respect and you can show people respect when you look at them in the eyes and that you like talking to them.

Question 2

Three-Point Response

If a reporter adds his or her own ideas to a story, then readers lose the ability to interpret the facts for themselves. By adding one's own ideas and interpretations to a news story, a reporter can lose credibility with the readers and skew the news story toward a particular bias. Facts must be reported objectively to allow them to speak for themselves. That way, a thoughtful, active reader can make an informed decision about the article's information based on the logical facts and not emotional bias of the reporter. That is, the facts must be the main focus or topic of the article in question and not the reporter's personal perceptions. By interjecting his or her personal opinions, the reporter shifts the focus of the article off of the article's principle subject or issue and on to the reporter him- or herself. Opinionated statements might result in an attraction of like-minded readers into agreement with the reporter, but those same personal opinions will repel contrary-minded or undecided individuals. Skewing the facts might also result in the astute reader questioning the reporter's motives or agenda, thus further reducing the reporter's legitimacy and credibility.

Two-Point Response

If a reporter adds their own ideas to a story then the entire news agency is at risk of appearing biased. The individual reporter's lack of objectivity will reflect on the news agency's overall image, and could result in a loss of subscribers or viewers. The audience could associate the news agency and such biased reporting as a form of "Yellow Journalism," and once this association between a news agency and unscrupulous tactics becomes planted in the public's mind, it could take years to restore the news agency's integrity, if the news agency can survive the public onslaught at all.

Additionally, a news agency which allows one reporter to present his or her personal opinions and interpretations of facts on any given topic is more likely to permit the other staff members with the "freedom" to present their biased judgments. So in this case, one bad apple really *can* spoil the whole barrel.

One-Point Response

It's really not good for reporters to tell what they think because no one really cares or wants to hear it anyway. Just like I'm sure a reporter doesn't really care about what I think so there is no reason for me to care about what they think. They are just reporters anyway, not political consultants or doctors or even college teachers. So what makes them think that they are experts on what they are reporting about anyway? It's not good for journalists to be unbiased about what they are reporting about because their opinions are like everyone else's and no one really wants to hear what they think. So they should just shut up and tell the story.

Question 3

Three-Point Response

Based on our primal animal instincts, like the hunting instincts of a lion or tabby, when our eye senses a moving object, on stage or elsewhere, our eye will instinctively follow and focus on that the movement. So, whether it's a character or an object, if the director wants to accent a particular character or object, the director can simply add motion to a "still scene" and the audience will collectively follow and focus on that person or object. Concurrently, if there are multiple characters or objects already in motion and the director does not want to stop the action already taking place, he or she can rely on our instincts to follow the newest or most recently animated character or object.

This same principle holds true for shifts in lighting as well. A shifting stage light will appear to the audience as a form of new movement and thus will have the same effect on the audience, as far as controlling audience focus is concerned. Since the shifting light is perceived by the eye as a new movement, the audience is instinctively compelled to follow that movement and focus on the character or object that the director wants us to look at.

Two-Point Response

Unlike a movie theater, where all the action takes place within the confines of a flat, rectangular screen, a theater's stage contains numerous nooks and crannies, offering numerous visual distractions. So, to attract the audience's attention to a particular object, area, or character on stage, the director should use movement, because movement is so "eye-catching," the audience can not help but follow it, as they attempt to focus on what is causing the movement. It doesn't matter if it's a person moving or some stage prop, the movement itself is enough to grab the audience's attention.

Several props or people in motion mean that important action is taking place on stage. Moving the lights from one prop or person to another, is like the person or prop moving itself, and has the same effect on the audience; causing their eyes to focus on the alternating spots of light on the stage.

One-Point Response

When it comes to moving things around on stage a director should be careful not to move too many things too fast or else the audience won't be able to follow what's going on in the play. I saw a play once that was like a three-ring circus, with so much going on at once that you didn't even know where to look first. It was really confusing and hard to follow. So, a good director should just move things around when it's absolutely necessary and not just for some action on the stage or the audience won't know where to look first.

Lights can be distracting too. If like they are flashing really fast, it can give me a headache and you can lose track of what your supposed to be following on the stage. So too many colored lights flashing and moving all at the same time can also be very distracting for the audience as well as the performers.

Question 4

Three-Point Response

The primary flaw with this draft is that the author "tells" rather than "shows" the dialog and action that is taking place between the couple. Dayton and Stella can and should be allowed to speak for themselves, rather than have a third-person narrator tell the reader what is going on in their conversation. Using direct quotes from their conversation will provide each of the two characters the opportunity to establish their individual voices. Additionally, allowing the reader to "listen in" on the couple's conversation provides insight into the characters personality traits. So, let us hear what Stella actually said to Dayton and the way she said it. That way, we will know exactly what "shocked (?)" Dayton so. This insight will in turn promote empathy on the part of the readers, allowing them to empathize with whichever character they most relate to. It will also give the draft a more active feeling, rather than the current "observational (lethargic) tone" it now uses.

Two-Point Response

The problem with the draft excerpt is that it uses too many vague generalities to describe the couple's actions and feelings. The author should use more concrete language to explain the troubles in the relationship. Instead of using an abstract phrase like "those awful things," the author could have told us that Stella "insulted" Dayton, or "announced that she was breaking up with him," or whatever the author meant by "awful things."

This revision would make the whole piece easier to understand, as it would be much easier for the reader to get a mental picture of the actual conflict(s) that are taking place between these two people. It would also give the reader a clearer insight into the characters by letting us know exactly what they think and feel.

One-Point Response

This draft would be much better if the people weren't fighting with each other. They should just sit down and calmly talk and get along better. Especially if it's his birthday! Its not very nice of her to insult him on his birthday, in fact, it's really rude! If she wanted to tell him she's pregnant or something, she should have waited until after his birthday to tell him. It's kind of sad that he can't even get to enjoy his birthday night, or go to the movie that he wanted to see. Maybe she caught him cheating with her friend and that's why she had to say something to him right then and there. If my boyfriend cheated on me I wouldn't care if it was his birthday or not either. So maybe she had a good reason to ruin his birthday. I think it would make more sense if that was the reason why she got mad at him on his birthday, and then as the reader, I could relate better to what's going and why the people are fighting.

Works Cited

Abrams, M. H. *A Glossary of Literary Terms*, 6th ed. Fort Worth, TX: Brace College Publishers, 1993.

Abrams, M. H., ed. The *Norton Anthology of English Literature*, 6th ed. Vols. 1 and 2. New York: W. W. Norton, 1993.

Baym, Nina. The *Norton Anthology of American Literature*, Shorter 4th ed. New York: W. W. Norton, 1995.

Beaty, Jerome. *The Norton Introduction to Literature*, Shorter 8th ed. New York: W. W. Norton, 2002.

Brown, Lesley. Shorter *Oxford English Dictionary*. New York: Oxford University Press, 1993.

Clouse, Barbara Fine. *Jumpstart: A Sentence-to-Paragraph Work Text with Readings*, 2nd ed. Boston: McGraw-Hill Publishers, 2007.

Crystal, David. *Encyclopedia of the English Language.* New York: Cambridge University Press, 1996.

Douglass, Frederick, essay "An Appeal to Congress for Impartial Suffrage" (*Atlantic Monthly*, 19, Jan. 1867: 112–117)

Finegan, Edward, *Language, Structure, & Use*, 2nd ed. Fort Worth, TX: Harcourt Brace, 1994.

Guralnik, David B. *Merriam-Webster's New World Dictionary*, 2nd College ed. New York: World Publishing, 1968.

Hacker, Diana. *The Bedford Handbook*, 6th ed. Boston: Bedford/St. Martin's, 2002.

Harris, Julian. *The Complete Reporter*, 4th ed. New York: Macmillan Publishing, 1981.

Hauser, Frank, *Notes on Directing*. New York: RCR Creative Press, 2003.

Morenberg, Max. *Doing Grammar*, 2nd ed. New York: Oxford University Press, 1997.

Strunk, William, and E. B. White. *The Elements of Style*, 4th ed. New York: Longman Publishers, 2000.

Stuart, Christina. *How to Be an Effective Speaker*. Chicago: NTC Publishing, 1993.

Thomas, A. J. *A Practical English Grammar*. New York: Oxford University Press, 1997.

WEBSITES AND ONLINE SOURCES CITED

American Literacy Council, *http://www.americanliteracy.com*.

Child Development Institute, LLC, *http://www.cdipage.com*.

Cornell University Cooperative Extension. "An Educator's Guide to Family Literacy." *http://www.parenting.cit.cornell.edu*.

Howard, E., Lindholm-Leary, K., Sugarman, J., Christian, D., and Rogers, D. *Guiding Principles for Dual Language Education*. Washington, DC: Center for Applied Linguistics, 2005. *http://www.cal.org*.

International Literacy Institute (ILI) and the National Center on Adult Literacy (NCAL). University of Pennsylvania Graduate School of Education, *http://www.literacy.org*.

Kentucky Literacy Partnership. "*Read to Succeed: Kentucky's Literacy Plan*." Kentucky Department of Education, *http://www.education.ky.gov*.

National Center for Family Literacy, 325 West Main Street, Suite 300, Louisville, KY 40202-4237; Phone: 502-584-1133; *http://www.famlit.org*.

National Institute for Literacy, *http://www.nifl.gov.*

North Central Regional Educational Laboratory, *http://www.learningpt.org.*

National Center for Education Statistics (NCES), *http://nces.ed.gov* (The NCES is located within the U.S. Department of Education and the Institute of Education Sciences, is the primary federal entity for collecting and analyzing data related to education.)

Purdue University Online Writing Lab (OWL), *http://owl.english.purdue.edu.*

University of Oregon, *http://grammar.uoregon.edu.*

Weinhold, Kellee. *"The Tongue Untied: A Guide to Grammar, Punctuation, and Style."* Edutopia, *http://www.edutopia.org.*

PRACTICE TEST 1: SUBTEST I

Abrams, *Glossary of Literary Terms*

Adams, Hazard. *Critical Thinking Since Plato*. Fort Worth, TX: Harcourt Brace College Publishers, 1992.

Crystal, *Encyclopedia of the English Language.*

Douglass, Frederick. "An Appeal to Congress for Impartial Suffrage." Electronic Text Center, University of Virginia Library, *http://etext.lib.virginia.edu.*

Frost, Robert. "The Figure a Poem Makes." In *The Norton Anthology of American Literature*, 5th ed. Vol. 2. New York: W.W. Norton, 1998.

Guralnik, *Merriam-Webster's.*

Hacker, *The Bedford Handbook.*

Harjo, Joy. "Call it Fear." In *Norton Anthology*.

Kafka, Franz. "A Hunger Artist." In *The Norton Introduction to Literature*, Shorter 8th ed. Edited by Jerome Beaty. Translated by Edwin and Willa Muir. New York: W. W. Norton, 2002.

Morenberg, *Doing Grammar*.

Strunk and White, *Elements of Style*.

North Central Regional Educational Laboratory

PRACTICE TEST 1: SUBTEST II

Brown, Shorter *Oxford*.

Crystal, *Encyclopedia of the English Language*.

Finegan, *Language, Its Structure*.

Guralnik, *Merriam-Webster's*.

Hacker, *The Bedford Handbook*.

Morenberg, *Doing Grammar*.

National Institute for Literacy

North Central Regional Educational Laboratory

Strunk and White, *Elements of Style*.

PRACTICE 1: SUBTEST III

Hughes, Langston. "Evenin' Air Blues." In *An Introduction to Literature: Fiction, Poetry, and Drama*, edited by Sylvan Barnet. New York: Pearson/Longman Press, 2000.

PRACTICE TEST 2: SUBTEST I

"Astrophel & Stella," Canto 1. In Abrams, *Norton Anthology*, Vol. 1.

Donne, John. "The Sun Poem." In *The Complete Poetry and Selected Works of John Donne*. New York: Random House, 1952.

Herrick, Robert. "Another upon Her Weeping." In *Hesperides or Works Both Human and Divine*. London: Routledge and Sons, 1884.

Melville, Herman. *Moby Dick or, The Whale*. Boston: Houghton Mifflin Co., 1956.

Shakespeare, William. Sonnet XVIII. In Abrams, *Norton Anthology*, Vol. 1.

Swift, Jonathan. *The Battle of the Books and Other Short Pieces*. 1727. Electronic book edited by Henry Morley. Project Gutenberg. *http://www.gutenberg.org*.

PRACTICE TEST 2: SUBTEST III

Blake, William. "The Chimney Sweeper." In *The Norton Anthology of English Literature*, 7th ed. Vol. 2. New York: W. W. Norton, 2000.

Emerson, Ralph Waldo. "Nature." In *The Norton Anthology of American Literature*, 5th ed. Vol. 1. New York: W. W. Norton, 1998.

Jokinen, Anniina. "The Life of Ben Jonson". *Luminarium*. 9 Sept 2003. *http://www. luminarium.org*.

Index

Installing REA's TEST*ware*®

SYSTEM REQUIREMENTS

Pentium 75 MHz (300 MHz recommended) or a higher or compatible processor; Microsoft Windows 98 or later; 64 MB available RAM; Internet Explorer 5.5 or higher.

INSTALLATION

1. Insert the CSET English CD-ROM into the CD-ROM drive.

2. If the installation doesn't begin automatically, from the Start Menu choose the RUN command. When the RUN dialog box appears, type d:\setup (where d is the letter of your CD-ROM drive) at the prompt and click OK.

3. The installation process will begin. A dialog box proposing the directory "Program Files\REA\CSET_English\" will appear. If the name and location are suitable, click OK. If you wish to specify a different name or location, type it in and click OK.

4. Start the CSET English TEST*ware*® application by double-clicking on the icon.

REA's CSET English TEST*ware*® is **EASY** to **LEARN AND USE**. To achieve maximum benefits, we recommend that you take a few minutes to go through the on-screen tutorial on your computer. The "screen buttons" are also explained here to familiarize you with the program.

TECHNICAL SUPPORT

REA's TESTware® is backed by customer and technical support. For questions about **installation or operation of your software**, contact us at:

> **Research & Education Association**
> **Phone: (732) 819-8880 (9 a.m. to 5 p.m. ET, Monday–Friday)**
> **Fax: (732) 819-8808**
> **Website: *www.rea.com***
> **E-mail: info@rea.com**

Note to Windows XP Users: In order for the TEST*ware*® to function properly, please install and run the application under the same computer administrator-level user account. Installing the TESTware® as one user and running it as another could cause file-access path conflicts.